Dedicated to –

This book is dedicated． best friend, and mentor. You were the greatest father life could have blessed me with. I miss you Daddy, but you will always be my angel - Fight On. Also, Brandon Carter, for showing me the insane world of the NFL I never thought I would see, and helping me realize what I was born to do.

Contents

Introduction IX
1. The Origins of Football 1
2. Fundamentals 5
   - 2.1 1. The Playing Field 5
   - 2.2 2. Scoring System 14
   - 2.3 3. Equipment 24
   - 2.4 4. Uniforms.. 44
   - 2.5 5. Personnel... 49
   - 2.6 6. Officiating.. 53
   - 2.7 7. The Season.. 64
3. Positions... 73
   - 3.1 The Offense 73
   - 3.2 Offensive Plays... 82
   - 3.3 The Defense 87
   - 3.4 Special Teams... 95
4. College Football 105
   - 4.1 High School Recruiting 106
   - 4.2 The NCAA: National Collegiate Athletics Association .. 110
   - 4.3 NCAA Clearinghouse 112
   - 4.4 Scandals and Sanctions 112
   - 4.5 Who Dominates Division-1..................... 122

    4.6   Polls *126*

    4.7   Bowls *127*

    4.8   BCS: Bowl Championship Series *128*

    4.9   All Americans *130*

5.   *The National Football League* **132**

    5.1   History of the NFL *133*

    5.2   AFL-NFL Merger 101 .... *134*

    5.3   The AFC *135*

    5.4   The NFC *146*

    5.5   Hall Of Fame *156*

    5.6   NFL Playoffs *157*

    5.7   The Pro Bowl *158*

    5.8   The Super Bowl *159*

    5.9   The Lombardi Trophy *160*

    5.10 The Draft Process *161*

    5.11 The NFL Draft *162*

    5.12 Free Agency *163*

    5.13 Rosters *165*

    5.14 Scandals, Controversies, and Issues *166*

6.   *The Canadian Football League* **176**

7.   *The Media* **180**

    7.1   Sideline Reporters *180*

   7.2   Football Analysts 181
8. Conclusion 184
9. Rules of Engagement 185
10. Glossary 189

Introduction

In my research for this book, I discovered several websites discussing game-day fashion, hygienic mishaps, Bartending 101, and recipes for the "perfect" game-day hors d'oeuvres. If that's what you're looking for, the only fashion literature you will ever need advice from is the fall issue of Vogue. For personal hygiene, I'm sure a round of martinis at your regular ladies nightspot will answer what your gynecologist can't. If you're having a hard time deciding how to harmonize your favorite spirits with juice, then chances are you were never in a sorority, so ask your friends on social media. Finally, if you're meticulously trying to plan a menu for game-day activities – whether it be a tailgate, or viewing party – let the men fire up the grill, and let your local grocery store take care of the rest.

This is football, this is life. This is a multi-billion dollar a year industry, and I assure you that your efforts to "look cute", or play "good little hostess" come game day, will only leave you on the bench.

All around the country, women complain that the men in their lives sit on their asses while their ladies slave away in the kitchens, and you might be one of them. Then the holidays come!

There's a movie called "The Blind Side", starring Sandra Bullock and Tim McGraw; it's a great film I suggest you all see, as it

~ Intro ~

accurately portrays the high school recruiting process for top prospects. In one of the scenes, Leigh Anne Tuohy (Bullock) notices Michael Oher eating at the dining room table by himself, while her kids and husband were in the living room watching the Ole Miss game with their Thanksgiving dinner. Think about how many times *your* holidays and dinner parties have been hijacked by football season. That's seven months of football, overlapped by other sports that "conflict" with the insanity of holidays and traditions we feel obligated to preserve. The truth is, in the forefront of our sane minds, we know that most of our families just want to bond over brews, booze, food and the Gridiron, in an informal way similar to the Tuohy's.

(Michael Oher was adopted by the Tuohy family where they changed his life. He received several scholarship offers but chose to attend the University of Mississippi {Ole Miss}. Oher was drafted in 2009 by the Baltimore Ravens in the 1st round, 23rd overall.)

To add insult to your already bruised ego, female sportscasters have taken the waves by storm, so while some of you are playing beermaid and personal cocktail waitress, your men are discussing Inez Sainz' ass, or which sportscaster/sideline reporter they would give anything to have married. But guess what? By not knowing the game, speaking the language, and holding your ground, you allow it!

I've had many discussions with men about this topic, and most of them would be elated if they knew their companion understood what was going on, could discuss big plays in the post, and hold their own. Many would agree that intelligence is a turn on anyway.

~ Intro ~

Planning the "perfect" menu, or wearing the sluttiest get-up to the tailgate confines women to the "dumb bitch" stereotypes that they need to sever ties with. So, if you want to be the perfect companion to your football die-hard, then be the total package, and learn the game yourself.

There are many women out there who are *very* well educated on the game, and can speak it with the best of them; if you consider yourself one, I salute you. If you're reading this to further elaborate what you know, and add to an existing repertoire, I promise this book will deliver.

My father always told me that I could never know too much about life; especially when it came to history, fine Cognacs, business, and football – lessons I apply in my everyday life, and throughout this book.

One of the (many) great things about the game of football, is how universal the language is, and how easy it is to understand once you have the basics down. In this book, I'll be breaking the mold to teach you the fundamentals of football, with several references that relate to you, the modern woman – from shopping, shoes, dating, drinking and more. So pour yourself a stiff one, and kick off your heels, *The Modern Girl's Guide to the Gridiron* is about to change the game of football as you know it.

Xo, VF

The Modern Girl's Guide to the Gridiron

VF Castro

Copyright © 2013 Vanessa-Franchesca Castro

All rights reserved.

ISBN-10: 1484872789

ISBN-13: 978-1484872789

Chapter One
The Origins of Football

Let's begin with this question: "Why is it called Football?"

Football is pretty much soccer's grandson, and as soccer evolved, certain rules like forbidding the use of your hands pissed some people off. In 1823 in England, a young lad named William Ellis picked the ball up with his hands on a play (ignoring all of the rules), and thus rugby – football's daddy – was born. Rugby eventually made its way overseas to the Ivy League, where it took on a whole new direction.

Fast forward:

The Rutgers Queensmen, and Princeton Tigers played a game on November 6, 1869, with rules that were very similar to rugby and soccer. But despite the formalities, it is considered the day that football was born in America.

In 1875, Harvard and Yale played their first football game together, which was still more of a hybrid game, involving both soccer, and rugby. Among the participants was Walter Camp, who had his own ideas about how the game should be played, and is credited as "The Father of American Football". In fact, the earliest recollections of American Football still favored advancing the football with your feet in many ways, and didn't even allow the forward pass.

~ The Origins of Football ~

Figure 1.1 - The Evolution of Football

Of course, when we think of football, the Ivy League falls well short of making SportsCenter highlights, or front-page news, but as previously stated, if it weren't for Harvard and Yale, the evolution would have likely sustained an impotent development.

Walter Camp is an important player in the evolution of the game, and you hear his name being used a lot, so it's important that you know who he is.

Camp was an ambassador for Yale – and the game itself – from his time there as a student (1876-1882), up until his death in 1925.

Notable additions to the sport, by Camp, were the safety (scoring), establishment of the line of scrimmage, down and distance, the forward pass, tackling, six-point touchdowns, offensive personnel – including the quarterback and center – the snap, and more. Camp was also a key player in the establishment of the National Collegiate Athletics Association (NCAA), though, by and large, most of the credit is given to the 26th President of the United States, Teddy Roosevelt (1901-1909).

~ The Origins of Football ~

Rules needed to be established because Ivy League, testosterone-driven males were killing each other on the field. If you're reading this, and you have a son (or daughter) who plays football, or would like to, but you're worried about them getting hurt, this section will be favored by your male counterpart, and I'm not apologizing.

When we think of the Ivy schools, we think of sweater vests, pressed khakis, and Sperry's-wearing properly refined East Coasters, but the 18th century was quite the antithesis to this stereotype. Football had zero governance back then, and players were out for blood. Every school seemed to have its own variation of the game, but Harvard and Dartmouth played something similar to the Battle at Gettysburg (American Civil War in 1863 in Pennsylvania) with a no-holds-barred beat down. The lawless game was highly protested and banned by Yale in 1860, with Harvard banning play in 1861. Gridiron casualties weren't really reported until 1905, in which there were 25 registered deaths due to football-related violence.

The modern translation of this chaos goes something like this: there are no rules to Black Fridays, and every single year, there are casualties and severe injuries as a result of Black Friday sales. Next November, imagine those $32.99 high-end, designer jeans are a football, and it's 1827. If that were the case, the "holiday" would be known as "Bloody Monday", and you'd likely be getting your ass beat over them. No flags, no encroachment calls; just you with a bloody face. If you think that football is "just a game", I can assure you that the man in your life says the same thing about your shopping: "It's just a (expletive) pair of overpriced jeans!"

~ The Origins of Football ~

The major difference is that in the NFL, if a player acts like an asshole, his check will be clipped to a ticket issued by the NFL Commissioner, (Officer) Roger Goodell; yet some women still call the sport, "barbaric". For the record, NFL checks are delivered by FedEx, so if you ever hear, or see anything relating to FedEx in the league, that's what it's referring to.

I'm not implying that all of you are like that, but you should understand how much football has evolved in terms of safety. Obviously, there have been deaths in the 21st century, but the next section on Fundamentals will explain everything you should know to help combat the risks involved.

Chapter Two
Fundamentals

This chapter is going to be an ass-kicking literary boot camp, so zone in and focus.

The Fundamentals of football are really quite simple:

1. The Playing Field
2. Scoring System
3. Equipment
4. Uniforms
5. Personnel
6. Officiating
7. The Season

1. The Playing Field

Let's start this section off, by saying that no two fields are created equal.

Most of you know what a domestic (American) football field looks like: 100-yards, broken down by 10-yard hash marks, starting at the 50-yard line which is centered, with two goal posts at the end of both endzones.

To be precise:

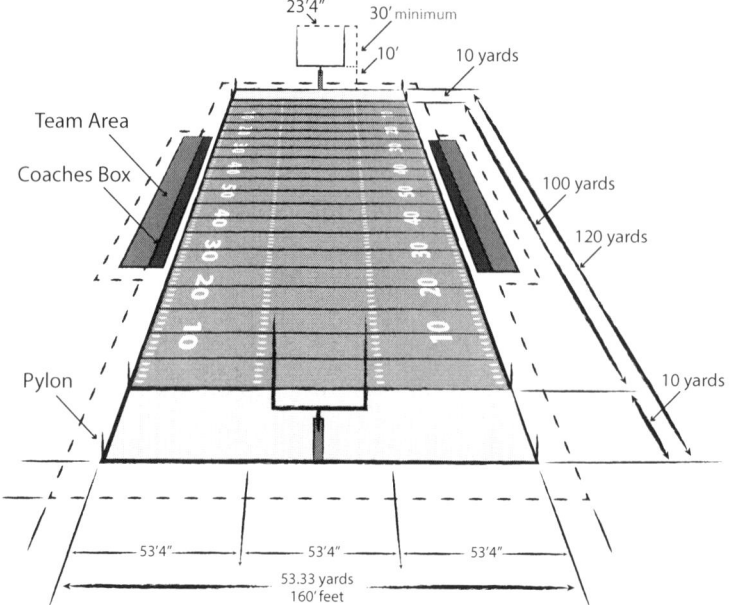

Figure 2.1 - Dimensions of a High School Football Field

~ Fundamentals ~

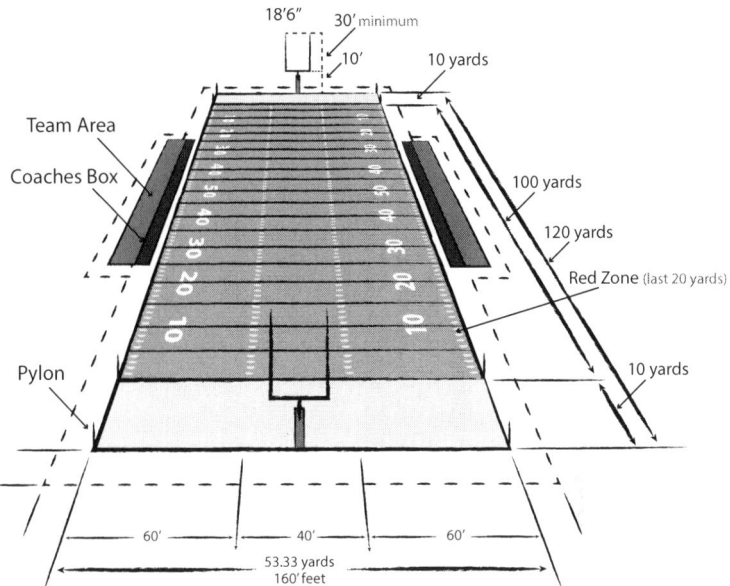

Figure 2.2 - Dimensions of an NCAA Field

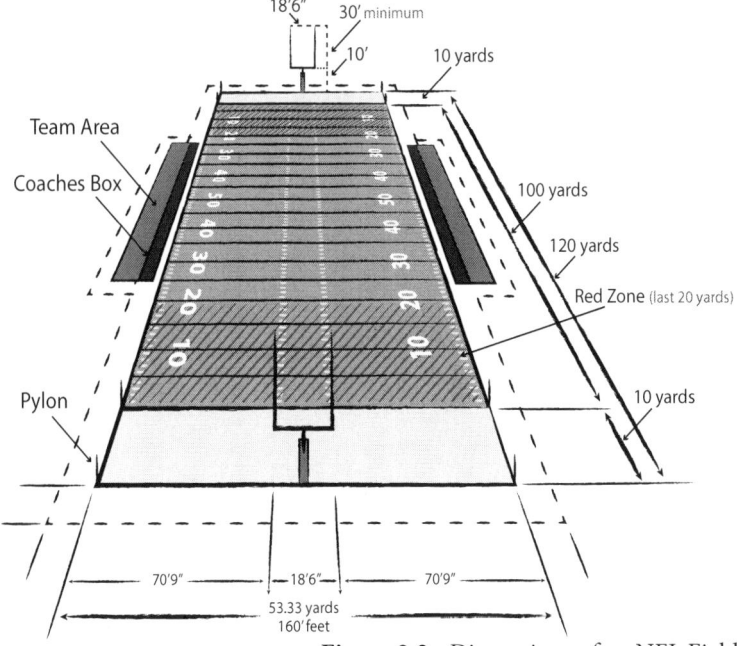

Figure 2.3 - Dimensions of an NFL Field

~ Fundamentals ~

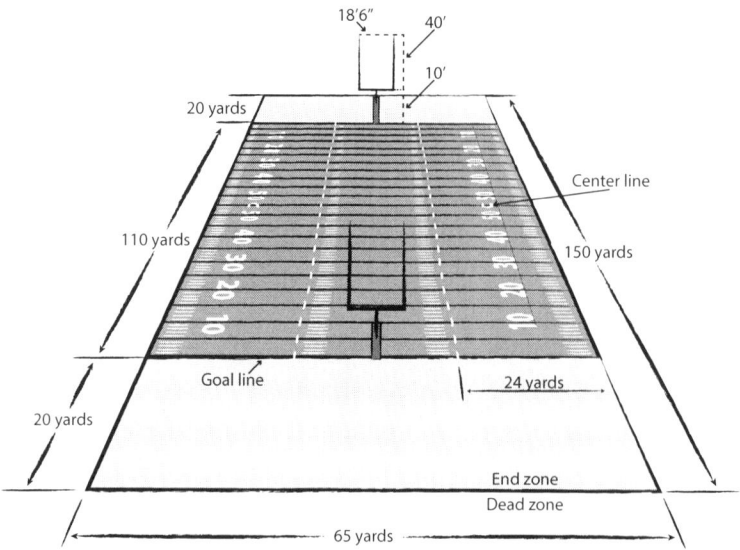

Figure 2.4 - Dimensions of a CFL Field

Field Colors

With the exception of painted endzones and logos on the field, the NFL doesn't allow teams to color their fields, but you will see it at two colleges. If you've ever watched College GameDay on ESPN, you've likely seen the infamous, and iconic "Smurf Turf" that is Bronco Stadium, home of the Boise State Broncos, who have posted an 84-4 record under head coach Chris Petersen from 2006, through 2012. The 1985 season was the last time the Broncos used standard green AstroTurf, with the 1986 debut of blue.

Eastern Washington University is another school following the trend with their majestic crimson approach, but unfortunately, Roos Field leaves a lot of critics seeing red, as the stadium is compared to that of a Texas high school field. But before you criticize, be advised. Roos Field was named after offensive tackle, Michael Roos, who graduated from E-Dub, and was selected 41st overall by the Tennessee Titans in the 2005 NFL Draft, so it has a pretty nice claim to naming rights fame. The stadium, dubbed "The Inferno", became the second colored college field in the country in 2009 when it upgraded to SprinTurf, via generous donations by ESPN personality, Colin Cowherd, and Roos – the three-time NFL Pro Bowler.

High schools from Alaska, to Texas have gradually started transitioning from the traditional green fields, but is the grass always greener on the other side? I say no, and while Boise State has had an impressive run on its Smurf Turf, the Broncos lost to the Texas Christian University Horned Frogs, 36-35 at home on November 12, 2011, and the San Diego State Aztecs, 21-19 on November 3, 2012. We can definitely say the Broncos should be cautious when it plays home games in November based on that statistic. Losses happen, shit happens. All that matters for teams playing on unfamiliar colored turf, is that they've spent all week in the film room studying their asses off, and that they're able to mute the noise. For high school teams, all I have to say is if the test scores aren't as high as the winning percentage, the money spent on sports programs would be better suited for classrooms.

Sure, it looks cool, but every Super Bowl, NCAA National Championship game, and high school championship game has been played on green turf, or grass; so as my father (and many before him) used to say, "If it ain't broken, don't fix it."

The only exception to this, is the Idaho Potato Bowl held every year at Bronco Stadium between Western Athletic Conference

(WAC), and Mid-American Conference (MAC) teams, but it's not a championship game, and there are no "home team" advantages, as Boise State is in the Mountain West Conference (MWC).

Climate

Climate and Altitude go hand-in-hand when preparing for a game, and you do see the two creating some level of problems for even the most elite of teams.

Based off weather alone, one might think the Indianapolis Colts (.525 all-time winning percentage, regular and post-season from 1953 - present) *should* have a better record than the Green Bay Packers (.566 from 1921-2012) because Lucas Oil Field is climate-controlled, and Indy gets an average of 27 inches of snow every winter, with an average summer high of 75 degrees, and a winter high of 26 degrees. In contrast, Green Bays' Lambeau Field is outdoors, and has an average snowfall of 47 inches, with a summer high of 81 degrees, and a winter high of 24 degrees.

Some might be new enough to watching football, following, or whatever the case, and they could be thinking: "The Colts aren't elite! They had the No. 1 overall 2012-draft pick! They suck... or did!" But the reason they "received" that top spot, was because of their 2-14, 2011 season. The Colts were 10-6 with quarterback Peyton Manning in 2010, but unfortunately, that season – and Manning's career with Indy – ended in a 17-16 Wild Card loss to the Jets. Yes. The Jets. However, Jets fans, 2013 NFL draft pick, quarterback Geno Smith promised a playoff run his rookie season!

~ Fundamentals ~

To help you stay on track, the Wild Card round in the NFL Playoffs, involves two teams from each division with the fifth, and sixth best records in the league. These teams play the third, and fourth place winners in their respective divisions, with the winners advancing to the Divisional Rounds. For example, in the American Football Conference (AFC), the third seeded (or third best record), would play the team with the fifth best record, or Wild Card No. 2.

Moving back to the Climate, let's take it to New Orleans, where the Saints always get shit during the playoffs for their climate-controlled Mercedes Benz Superdome. With the exception of a dismal 7-9 record in 2012, since winning Super Bowl XLIV in 2010, the Saints won the NFC-South Division every year, yet lost on the road during the Playoffs at Seattle in 2010, and San Francisco in 2011.

What happened during Hurricane Katrina, and why did the levees break? The city is up to 10-feet-below sea level, lies at the inland heart of the Gulf of Mexico, and is subject to (as we've seen), catastrophic hurricane damage. If you've ever been to Mexico, or any coastal city near the Gulf of Texas, to Florida, what are the things you notice? Moisture dripping through the vents in your car, excessive sweat, your hair gets frizzy, your lungs have to work harder to breath, and the hangover is a heck of a lot worse than say, Las Vegas – which is equally as hot. Why is that? Humidity. Imagine that sort of climactic change for an athlete who has to play in it. You get used to it living there, but what if you're on the road? An NFL team such as the Oakland Raiders, which visits the New Orleans Saints in 2013, is given a significant advantage, because it doesn't have to play in a climate it is unfamiliar with. This is why the weather reports are so closely monitored and listed before games. Also, keep in mind that weather and wind significantly effect how the football travels.

From frigid, snowy weather that leaves your lips frostbitten, to the type of heat, and humidity that burns your eyes, and leaves you fatigued for days after, weather is part of the game. Some teams prefer climate-controlled environments because it creates a relatively smooth game, whereas, others prefer to take the climate head on. Sure, your team might get flagged for a *False Start, or *Encroachment because they can't hear the snap count in a closed stadium, but next time someone bitches about the Dome, ask how their team would fare playing – and cramping – in a city below sea level, with a yearly relative humidity of 76 percent. And for the record, it can snow in New Orleans, too.

Vocabulary

- **12th Man**: Jumping way back in the history books, the 12th MAN was initially referenced in 1903, when E.A. McGowan wrote an article for his school's newspaper (The Iowa Alumnus) to describe the fans in a game between the University of Iowa (then State University of Iowa), and the University of Illinois.

  The Texas A&M Aggies (Southeastern Conference, or SEC) documented the 12th MAN on January 2, 1922, when TAMU (then, The Agricultural & Technical College of Texas) was playing defending champion, Centre College in the National Championship game. Due to a thinning roster plagued by injuries, coach D.X. Bible brought in E. King Gill (who left the team at the end of the regular season for basketball) to dress out in case they needed him. Although Gill never played, he became known as the 12th Man. TAMU trademarked the term in December 1989, which was approved in September 1990, by the United States Patent and Trademark Office.

When the Seahawks debuted in Seattle in 1976, the city erupted overnight with legions of fans, whose main goal was to be the most obnoxiously loud crowd in league history, and in the 80s, they succeeded. This level of insanity introduced the 12th MAN – which was the number dedicated to the fans, as they contributed "volumes" in terms of distracting visiting teams, and throwing off offenses with their noise. The most notorious account of this happened on November, 27, 2006, where the crowd noise played a major role in the New York Giants committing 11 false start penalties, as well as forcing kicker Jay Feely to miss three field goals. In 2006, Texas A&M filed a trademark suit against the Seahawks that was settled out of court, and allowed the franchise to use the phrase, as long as the Aggies were acknowledged as the proprietor league-wide, and received monetary compensation.

- *False Start* (against the offense): when a member of the Offense moves after taking his set position, and before the ball is snapped. This results in a 5-yard penalty and play is stopped.

- *Encroachment (against the defense)*: when a defensive player crosses the Line of Scrimmage prior to the snap and makes contact with an offensive player. This results in a 5-yard penalty and play is stopped.

- *Offsides (against the defense):* when a defensive player crosses the line of scrimmage before the ball is snapped. The defensive player has the opportunity to get back on his side of the line, and must do so prior to the snap. If he is too slow and the ball is snapped, the penalty is called, and the play resumes. This is a free play for the offense.

~ Fundamentals ~

- *Free Play*: this occurs when the defense has committed an infraction that negates the results of that particular play. Basically, if the offense fails do something productive, they can "accept" the penalty and benefit that way. If, on the other hand, they were to score a touchdown for example, they would "decline" the penalty and take the points.

  Believe it or not, coaches have declined this, and theorists will always say that it has to do with "The House", which refers to Vegas betting lines and point shaving.

- *Neutral Zone Infraction (against the defense)*: when a defensive player jumps offside and causes an offensive player to commit a false start. This is held against the defense resulting in a 5-yard penalty, and play is stopped.

2. Scoring System

Scoring at any level of play is universal:

- *6 points are awarded for a Touchdown;*
- *1 point is awarded for the Extra Point attempt immediately following, or if a team is bold:*
- *2 points for a two-point conversion;*
- *2 points are given for a Safety;*
- *3 points for a Field Goal.*

Here are explanations of all five scoring instances, with references to some of the greatest point-scoring plays in recent history:

~ Fundamentals ~

The Touchdown

The touchdown is always the main objective for an offense; It's good for six points, and provides an opportunity for the team to go for one, or two more points. A touchdown is scored when the ball – under legal possession – crosses the goal line, and into the endzone, or rectangular shaped space filled with the team name or logo.

- *For a player to have legal possession, the ball must be controlled by the player with his hands, and stay in bounds.*

One of the best touchdowns was scored by Marshawn "Beast Mode" Lynch of the Seattle Seahawks, during the 2010 Season Wild Card Playoff game win versus the New Orleans Saints. Here's the quick download on Lynch: He's a Running Back out of California (Berkley), drafted 12th overall in the 1st Round by the Buffalo Bills. Lynch – a three time Pro Bowler (which we'll go over in the NFL Chapter), has scored 46 career TDs, and was voted No. 24 in the "Top 100 Players of 2013." With that said, it's a no-brainer that he's pretty damn good, so the play I'm about to describe shouldn't come as a shock.

On January 8, 2010, Seattle quarterback Matt Hasselbeck handed the ball off to Lynch around the Seattle 29-yard line, with 3:37 in regulation, and four seconds on the play clock. Lynch ran up the middle (thanks to picture perfect blocking by the Seattle offensive line) 67-yards, shedding tackles by New Orleans' finest: Scott Shanle, Darren Sharper, Remi Ayodele, Jabari Greer, and Tracy Porter, and danced into the endzone for a Skittles-earning celebration that registered seismic activity 100 miles away from CenturyLink Field.

If you watch a Seahawks game, you'll see that when Lynch scores, he's rewarded with Skittles – a tradition started by his mother when he was younger. Lynch is also the proud "sole" owner of custom "Skittles" Nike cleats.

Extra Point: PAT or Point After Touchdown

After scoring a touchdown, a team is given the option to kick for an extra point. This is the most common and safest option, where the kicker from the scoring team must kick the ball through the goal post (between the uprights, and over the crossbar). This is also easier said, than done. The PAT is allowed even if the game clock has expired, with the exception of Sudden Death Overtime instances.

In Sudden Death, there is a universal rule of ending the game immediately following an initial scoring situation.

It should be noted that in the NFL, if no points have been scored after the first OT, the game ends in a tie. This has only happened 18 times in League history, with the most recent instance, a 24-24 tie, that happened on November 11, 2012, between the 49ers and the St. Louis Rams in San Francisco.

Along the lines of clock expiration, the clock <u>does not</u> continue during PAT's or Conversions. The play clock continues to tick, and the offense has 25 seconds to get the ball snapped, or else risk Delay of Game penalties, which can push an offense back five-yards.

~ Fundamentals ~

Extra Points: 2-Point Conversion

This is the second option a team has at scoring additional points immediately following a TD.

Conversions are worth two points (duh), but there's a risk involved with "going for it." For starters, the completion rating for conversions averages less than 40 percent. Suppose your team is down by one point, having just scored a TD with 12 seconds left in the fourth quarter. Your coach is put in a predicament of deciding whether to go for that game-winning "8th" point, or stay conservative and accept the PAT, which will usually send the game into overtime.

- *The only level of play where the conversion is mandatory after a TD, is on the college level,when the game goes into Triple Overtime.*

- *In High School and the NFL, the play is blown dead after a turnover on the extra point attempt. College, on the other hand, allows the advancement of the football after a turnover, which makes for a more exciting game, if you ask me.*

Ball placement during extra point attempts:

	NFL	NCAA	CFL	Semi-Pro
Ball Placement	2-Yard Line	3-Yard Line	5-Yard Line	3-Yard Line

Example:

- In reference to the mandatory college Triple OT, the

~ Fundamentals ~

best game to explain this happened in the 2011 season. On October 29, the No. 6 nationally ranked Stanford Cardinal – led by Heisman candidate runner-up Andrew Luck, took on the USC Trojans, at the Los Angeles Memorial Coliseum, in what was quite possibly the most badass game of the entire college season. Let's fast forward to triple overtime. Stanford was driving, and on 1st & Goal, RB Stepfan Taylor ran the ball in for a TD; since it was triple OT, Stanford had to attempt the 2-point conversion. Luck converted on a pass to Coby Fleener to top USC, 22-14 in total OT points. USC fired back strong when QB Matt Barkley hit freshmen WR, Marqise Lee (USC's first Biletnikoff Award winner in 2012) on a 21-yard pass setting the Trojans up to convert. On USC's 2-point attempt, RB Curtis McNeal gave up a costly fumble on the 4-yard line, sending the football into the endzone, where it was recovered by No. 44, Stanford redshirt Junior Linebacker Chase Thomas. Per CFB rules, remember, if that fumble had been recovered by USC, it would have been a successful conversion, and the game would have gone into an unprecedented 4OT.

Translation: Say you're at a bar in Austin, TX when the bartender yells "Last Call!" at 1:45AM, and after a few minutes, you stumble to the bar where you order another drink. It takes you 15 minutes to move the distance markers on your high ball, but at 2am, you realize that your six-ounce (TD) cocktail still didn't make you drunk enough to pursue your Unrestricted Free Agency status (single), so you try ordering a shot where you're turned down; you're bitch-slapped with defeat, and your eyes well up in drunken tears. Translating that into football shouldn't be hard, as most of us have been there. Imagine thinking (with your drunk, distorted perception of time) that last ounce (or point) of sweetness is attainable – you can even see it on the shelf! The same general concept of defeat runs through a football player's mind, when no matter how hard he went, for however long the game lasted, it just wasn't enough. The only difference between you, and say Curtis McNeal, is that you and your shit-kickers can giddy up to Gatti's next to Kung Fu Saloon on W. 6th for pizza and a cab, and forget the night happened. The "McNeal's" out there *get* (sarcastic emphasis) to relive the anguish for the next week – or longer – depending on if it's say… a National Championship game.

That sticks, hard, and could be a highlight on the "Intangibles List" when that player decides to declare for the Draft.

Safety

There are two kinds of Safeties in Football: one is a defensive skill position, that we'll cover in the Personnel section, but in terms of scoring, a Safety occurs when either the respective ball carrier (typically the quarterback) is downed in his own endzone, or there is an offensive foul committed in a team's own endzone. An offensive foul can be a number of things, which I'll go over in the Officiating section.

How does a team get pushed that far back? It's the job of the kicking team to try and down the ball as close to the opposing teams endzone as possible. Remember: *The more distance an offense has to cover, the less likely they are to score.*

If the ball goes into the opposing endzone, the offense starts on its own 20-yard line, so you will never see a drive begin in an opposing endzone; this is called a Touchback.

~ Fundamentals ~

- One of the greatest Safety Moments happened in Super Bowl XLVI, where New York Giants Punter, and six-year Veteran out of Illinois, Steve Weatherford set up the Giants' notorious quad-shot arsenal of Jason Pierre-Paul, Justin Tuck, Mathias Kiwanuka, and Osi Umenyiora for a perfect defensive opening drive by downing the ball on the Patriots' five-yard line. (Quad Shot meaning, two Defensive Ends, and two Defensive Tackles. In SB XLVI, the Giants rode dirty on Tom Brady in the *Pass Rush with three DE's and one DT.) To avoid the sack on the opening drive, Brady lobbed the ball 50-yards down field… into a pile of open turf. The Officials ruled his "pass" as Intentional Grounding – which is exactly what it sounds like: a pass intended for nobody, because there are no offensive players in the area where the ball is thrown. Despite commotion on the sidelines and in the crowd, there was absolutely no way to refute the ruling, and again, because the IG call was an offensive foul, the ruling resulted in a Safety, giving the Giants a 2-0 lead.

This was only the sixth safety in the history of the Super Bowl, and only the second time in Super Bowl history that there was a 2-0 score. The first happened on January 12, 1975 in SB IX (Tulane University, New Orleans, LA), where Steelers' Defensive End, Dwight White sacked Vikings' QB, Fran Tarkenton in the second quarter. The Steelers won their first Super Bowl, 16-6 that day.

In the 2013 Fiesta Bowl between the Oregon Ducks (Pac 12) and Kansas State (Big 12), the Wildcats blocked an Oregon extra point, recovered the ball, then attempted to cut back and run it out of the endzone. They failed, so the ball-carrier flipped it to another player who was tackled in the endzone, which resulted in a one-point safety – or the equivalent of an extra point. If you ever have to hear an awkward and "unique situation" unfolding, you better hope that college football official Ron Cherry is the one delivering.

~ Fundamentals ~

The Field Goal

The Field Goal (FG) is a way for the offense to score some points. It's basically a kick, just like the PAT, except they can try it from anywhere on the field, assuming they're close enough. Better kickers give you longer range, and therefore, are worth their weight in gold. Typically, you'll see field goal attempts when an offense has failed to score a touchdown, or convert on downs and face a fourth down situation, provided the kick can be made within the kickers' range. If not, the ball is usually punted away.

Being that they are only worth three points, field goals aren't as good as touchdowns, but in a game where inches make all the difference, every little bit counts.

What happens when the ball flies higher than the tips of the posts? The Luxor Hotel and Casino in Las Vegas, Nevada has a light beam at the top of the pyramid; now imagine that same beam of light shooting up from the tips of every field goal post in the country. During a field goal or extra point (XP or PAT), if the ball would have been inside the "beams", it is declared a score.

In Arena Football, if the PK dropkicks the ball and hits it, it's worth two-points, otherwise it's worth one. The popularity of dropkicking ended around 1934, when the sport adopted the prehistoric version of its current oblong shaped football. Before that, it had similar features of a soccer ball, and could be easily kicked, with greater accuracy.

~ Fundamentals ~

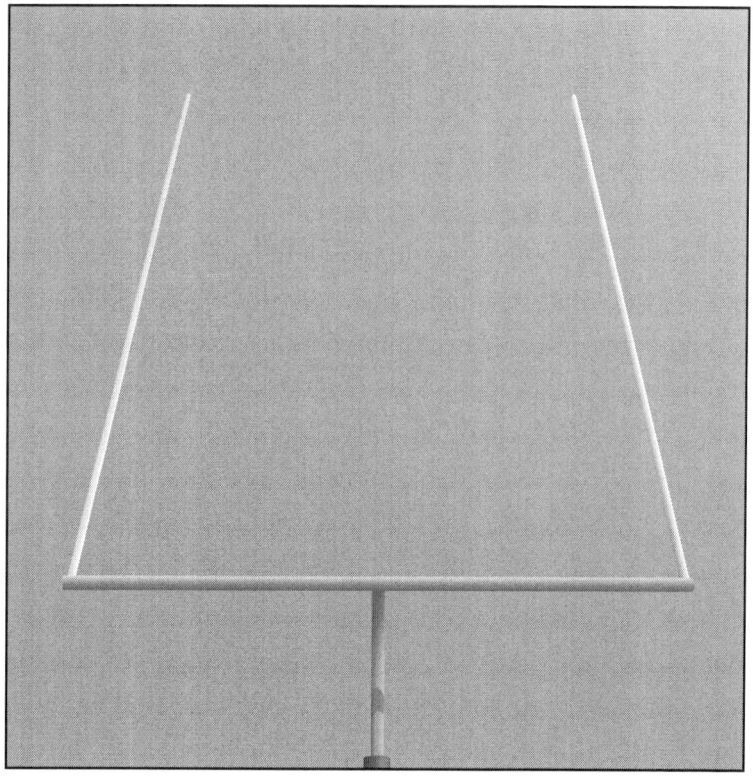

Figure 2.5 - Field Goal Posts

~ Fundamentals ~

Vocabulary

- *Move The Chains*: an archaic – yet indisputable – unit of measuring 10-yard increments, starting at the original Line of Scrimmage. The Chains are located on the sidelines, and carried by personnel in orange vests with vertical stripes, or argyle print. Think of a caddy at a golf course, minus the tumultuous task of selecting which Iron would best serve Tiger Woods' chip shot.

The Chain Gang carries one chain set measuring 10-yards, and one down box, so yes, while this important group of gentlemen don't have the capabilities of f***ing up the course of the game, they do have fans wanting to throw their beers at them if their chains come up short on downs. So, if you've ever wondered how players on the field know where they stand on down and distance, now you know.

The chains come on the field when the spot where the ball last touched needs to be confirmed.

- *Pass Rush*: When defensive players attempt to get to the quarterback and tackle him, before he makes a pass.

~ Fundamentals ~

Figure 2.6 - The Chain Gang

3. Equipment

In this section, we will be covering the anatomy of the football itself, to what's under the jersey – boxer briefs, and jock straps included!

~ Fundamentals ~

The Football

Figure 2.7 - An American Football

Every ball used in the NFL has been manufactured in Ada, Ohio – home of the Wilson Factory – who has been the single supplier of league balls since 1941. Wilson also supplied most NCAA programs since 1955, but in the summer of 2013, the University of Michigan Wolverines decided to take its rivalry with the Ohio State Buckeyes up a notch, by introducing Adidas footballs cleverly stamped, "Made in USA – Not In Ohio."

The official NFL football is called "The Duke", and provides for better air retention, moisture control, and has a firmer texture for improved grip. This is also the largest of the footballs, but its size is approved for high school-level of play, up to the pros.

If you haven't seen the movie "Varsity Blues", I suggest you do so as soon as possible. In the film, Jonathan Moxon's (James van der Beek) father says "… fire that f***ing pigskin." Why is this important? Well, footballs aren't made of "pigskin"; they're made of cowhide, usually taken from the back of the cow, or a steer.

The reason footballs were called pigskins, is that the earliest versions were made of inflated pig bladders, which were later covered by leather, then phased out entirely and replaced with rubber, and other flexible materials.

Equipment and Safety

Call it what it is, the first thing we notice when we watch football, are the tattoos, tight butts, biceps, and tightly fitted jerseys over abs so chiseled you could run a six-way tequila luge on. But the reality is, uniforms aren't designed for our "Magic Mike" visual exploits, but rather to maximize players' aerodynamics, movement, and protect their bodies – at any cost.

I'm throwing an *Audible from Helmets through Knee Pads because safety is the most important factor of the game, and I want to stress that these sections aren't intended to stimulate your senses through witty explanations or perversions. But don't worry, we will be having the jock strap versus boxer brief debate upon the conclusion of Knee Pads.

Vocabulary

- ***Audible***: When the play is changed at the line of scrimmage.

The basic protective layers under the uniform usually consist of the following components:

~ Fundamentals ~

Figure 2.8 - Protective Pads & Safety Equipment

Helmets and the Facemask

Let's take it from the top with Helmets. Composites are fairly universal, as they are simply a hard, plastic shell with foam-rubber padding on the insides, and a chin-strap to keep it secured to the player's head. They are designed to protect players from concussions and other head injuries.

~ Fundamentals ~

Figure 2.9 - Football Helmet

We've all worn helmets for various activities, so explaining the safety reasons would be a waste of your time. I will say, however, that football helmets don't protect against concussions. In fact, as more rules enforcing safety are drawn up and implemented throughout the leagues and the NCAA, the more researchers have confirmed that modern helmets are no safer than the "Leatherhead" variation dating back to the 1920's – when protection started being addressed as a necessity. While this is an extensively researched fact, Leatherheads also lacked Facemasks, which was a huge safety advancement.

Modern helmets provide a significantly higher level of

protection against high-impact collisions, but "mild" head-to-head hits can still result in a myriad of neurological issues and structural damages, so I absolutely do not advise slicing a football in half and strapping it to your head with duct tape as a cheaper alternative; although I strongly encourage this as a Halloween costume.

Heated discussions among men about rules changes to combat Helmet-To-Helmet hits are the norm these days, and there really is no way to avoid the issue. Unfortunately, year after year, players become victims to life altering gridiron decisions that – in severe cases – can lead to paralyzation.

One of the most frequently discussed instances of paralyzation from an H-to-H occurred on October 16, 2010, when Rutgers' defensive tackle Eric LeGrand dropped his shoulders in an attempt to tackle Army's Malcolm Brown on a kickoff return. LeGrand rolled onto the 35-yard line, with 5:13 left in the fourth quarter at New Meadowlands Stadium in a play that forever changed his young life.

That play isn't uncommon, and if a player leads into a tackle with his helmet or spears his opponent, the penalty automatically results in 15-yards and a 1st down for the opposing team.

While discussing safety, it should be noted that around 265 players have been paralyzed from spinal chord injuries since 1977. As of 2012, it was reported that 62 percent of bankruptcies were attributed to medical bills, and according to CNN.com, 16.3 percent (49.9 million) of the US population doesn't have health insurance. Since this book is targeted towards women, I also want to throw it out there, that in May 2013, MSNBC's Jane

C Timm, reported that a record 40 percent of U.S. households were being supported fully, or primarily by working moms with a median family income of $17,000.

Education is stressed intently in this book as a way to make people aware of the things that *could* happen in football, so before signing waivers of any kind, please make sure that at the high school level (when play is rough, and athletes are vying for scholarships), and at the collegiate level, you ask about Catastrophic Insurance Policies to make sure that should anything happen, your loved ones are covered so you, or your family members don't fall victim to financial disaster.

There's a film called "Head Games" directed by Steve James, that is based on the book of the same title by former WWE star and Ivy League football player, Chris Nowinski, that I highly recommend. It provides compelling research and interviews discussing all the issues surrounding concussions and neurological trauma athletes can sustain in all sports.

Facemasks

In the diagram above, you can see that the Facemask is attached to the outer plastic shell of the helmet by four, or more screws. Players like New York Giants defensive end, Justin Tuck have taken the design elements to a whole new level with his Megatron/Transformers-inspired facemask. But traditionally, it consists of several rubber coated bars along the mouth, nose, and sides, to prevent facial injuries. We can analyze this feature all day, but I know you'd much rather shift focus to the undergarments.

Vocabulary

- *Helmet-To-Helmet Hit*: an illegal act, when two helmets collide with emphasized target on a defenseless player. This is illegal at the high school level, with all forms made illegal outright by the NCAA in 2005. The NFL levies heavy fines from $2,500 (San Francisco 49ers WR Michael Crabtree on October 15, 2010) and up, with the possibility of player suspensions. Former Steelers' Linebacker James Harrison (who is easily one of the best in the game), threatened retirement, after he was fined $75,000 for an H-to-H on Cleveland Browns' WR Mohammad Massaquoi in October 2011. Harrison, among many other defensive players, continue to battle the NFL on their ever-evolving rules changes, they strongly feel favor the offense and scoring, which interferes with how the defense is allowed to do its job.

    Harrison, who is now a Cincinnati Bengal, is definitely one of the nastiest players in the league, but one who you should respect regardless of who your favorite team is, because he stands strong in defending the old school flow of professional football.

- *Spearing*: is the intentional use of a helmet and facemask to hurt an opponent.

Shoulder Pads

Like many of the older versions of equipment, shoulder pads were initially made of leather, and were exactly that. This trend in fashion didn't begin on the Parisian runways in the 1980s, however. It began around 1890, when leather pads were sewn into the jersey itself. This method provided little protection, but did spawn an inventive intrigue by sporting goods manufacturers to create the ancestors to what we see today.

The invention process took around 80 years for designers to finally replace leather with plastic, but imagine wearing a 10-pound layer on your skin, under a thick (sometimes polyester) jersey while playing against hot, unforgiving conditions.

Perhaps, the vast number of deaths by likely BPA skin intoxication, and incineration was enough for those same pioneers to go back to the drawing boards, and the 1960s were a perfect time to do so.

The era in fashion was most notorious for its synthetics, so they were integrated into the padding, separating shoulder pads from skin. As time went on, the plastic became even lighter, and foam inserts were added.

Modern shoulder pads are made of shock absorbing foam, and plastic technology that are designed specifically for different positions, as the levels of shock that players sustain are considerably different.

In 2004, researchers at the University of Florida College of Medicine, revolutionized the way athletes performed against the harsh Southern conditions, by developing a pad designed to regulate a players' body temperature. If you haven't heard of this before, or haven't paid attention to the sideline before, look closely this season at the benches; players come off the field and get hooked into machines that can cool body temperatures down significantly without adding weight, or hindering movement.

I want to add that researchers at the University of Florida also developed Gatorade in 1965 (hence the mascot "Gators") as a quick way to restore electrolytes, carbohydrates, sodium, and potassium during intense practices and games. The original flavor was the classic Lemon-Lime, and since then, the product has launched an all-out assault to combat fatigue, exhaustion, and depletion with its G-Series line.

So, if you're a die-hard fan of an SEC team who rivals the Gators – or Ohio State – and you see the product on your sideline, remember that in 1967, following a 27-12 loss to Florida in the Orange Bowl, Georgia Tech Yellow Jackets' coach Bobby Dodd said, "We didn't have Gatorade. That made the difference."

If you're in college, or you're a young adult and reading this, insane amounts of money and research have gone into a social science experiment that pounding vodka and Gatorade, or "Faderade" can prevent and/or reduce hangovers. I was on that panel – many times – and it's a ruse. I know, bummer.

It's important to throw the Collar in here, because protecting the neck is just as important as the head, and a lot of football injuries are shoulder related, and initiated by contact with the players' neck. The collar fits around the neck like a scarf would, except it's usually made of a contoured shock absorbing foam covered by vinyl, or another light material. A Neck Roll is similar, and it's basically a thick piece of foam that snaps onto shoulder pads. They've been phased out on the professional level since the 1990s, as new equipment has taken its place. But if you're a mom worried about *Burners or *Stingers and maximizing protection without your child looking like nostalgic conversation piece, their coach should be able to recommend something more modern.

Vocabulary

- *Horse-Collar Tackle*: when a defender (not to be confused with a member on the defense) tackles his opponent by grabbing the back of his neck between the helmet and shoulder pads/collar area; this does include the jersey itself. The NFL was the first to ban this in 2005, with the NCAA following in August 2008, citing that its intent was to reduce back injuries, and the high school level by 2009. At every level of play, the penalty for a Horse Collar results in a loss of 15-yards for the team committing the infraction. A lot of analysts and seasoned fans will bring up former Dallas Cowboys' safety Roy Williams when HCT's are committed, because he is considered to be the reason why the NFL pulled the trigger after the 2004 season, outlawing them altogether. The retired five-time Pro Bowler successfully, and severely inflicted three opponents in the 2004 season, making the penalty referred to as, "The Roy Williams Rule."

  I think it's safe to say that anyone who has had their hair, weave, or extensions pulled on, is familiar with the whiplash/neck jerking effect, and this is similar to what a horse collar feels like.

- *Burner/Stinger*: is when the network of nerves along the spinal chord stretch, or compress, causing sharp pains and a tingle that extends across the shoulder and down to the arms, but never both at the same time. This causes numbness and weakness, but is typically isolated and disappears after a few minutes. We've all had them, and the closer you pay attention to injuries that occur during games, you'll realize that several of the minor injuries are burners/stingers. They aren't serious, however, in standard protocol, if the pain continues or gets worse, a doctor should be seen immediately.

Rib Guards/Flack Jackets/Rib Pads

Rib Guards are exactly that. In Lacrosse, the Shoulder Pads and Rib Guards are usually one solid piece, but always remember that in football, the equipment varies by position. Rib guards are typically a light, shock absorbing foam (see the trend here?) on a plastic composite shell, with snaps that connect to the back of the shoulder pads. Flack Jackets are a made with similar components, except they have straps like a vest, that cross in the back.

Rib Pads and Protectors come in either a thin, but highly durable Muscle-T, or short sleeve shirt, and have a moisture wicking technology to keep the player dry, as well as body cooling technology. These shirts have five pieces: a spine pad, two shoulder pads, and two rib pads.

Hip Pads/Thigh Pads

Next to pulled hamstrings, quadriceps and hips top the list when it comes to what spectators view as "no big deal" injuries. On the contrary, these injuries – if untreated – can, and will result in severe complications.

Many trials and tests have been conducted to further technological advances in prevention, but the truth is that a players' most credible source of knowledge, comes from their coaches, trainers, and specialists.

The first step is to make sure the pads are fitted and placed in the appropriate areas. Most sporting goods stores sell a one-size-fits-all set that is designed to protect *hip flexors and the lower waist. But as we all know, one-size-fits-all doesn't usually work out, and should be overseen by a specialist to ensure a perfect fit. Much like a suit you need altered, if you were unsure of the measurements, you would take it to a tailor.

The second step is making sure they are placed into the pockets allocated for them on the sides – in the correct pant size – that starts slightly above the natural waist, down to the bottom of the players' butt. The sizes of football pants don't vary drastically, but should allow for structurally sound padding.

Let's move on to thigh pads. Football players actually have their own form of a girdle, which connects all the lower extremity "safety dots." These shorts are designed with shock plate padding for hips, tailbones, and thighs, which eliminate pad removal; they're practically Spanx. The only difference between women's girdles and men's, is that the female variety is strictly for vanity purposes, while men's are for athletic usage, so you can't take jabs at guys for wearing them.

Much like all of the equipment discussed, there is a second option of loose pads, which come as a "snap-in", or "slotted" variation. Snap-In's are just that, while slotted pads slide into the pockets designated for them on the thigh part of the pants, with the curved (or bulging) side facing outward.

In the world of football, injuries can't be avoided entirely, but every ounce of safety needs to observed and addressed. In September 2011, New Orleans Saints' Kicker Garrett Hartley – who was a huge part in the Saints' Super Bowl Run the year prior – was sidelined for several months due to an injured hip flexor in a PAT versus the Oakland Raiders. All it takes is one split second to end a season, so never be a smartass when it comes to any injury that occurs during a game, and always be aware of any symptoms.

Vocabulary

- *Hip Pointers*: are usually caused by tackling, which results in a bone bruise, or in more serious cases, a fracture to the pelvis. This can be felt on the iliac crest, which is the bony area along the waist. When this injury is sustained, the best method of treatment is to ice the area, and take anti-inflammation medications, but in severe cases, X-Ray's are required, followed by physical therapy.

- *Hip Flexors*: are the three muscles that give flexion to the hip: the Rectus Femoris (hip to femur), Psoas Major (spine to femur), and Illiacus (hip bone to femur). If severe trauma occurs, the player will experience excruciating pain, but rest, ice, and therapy to restore flexibility can usually treat the injury. While this seems minor, remember that all injuries are not created equal, and should never be treated as such.

~ Fundamentals ~

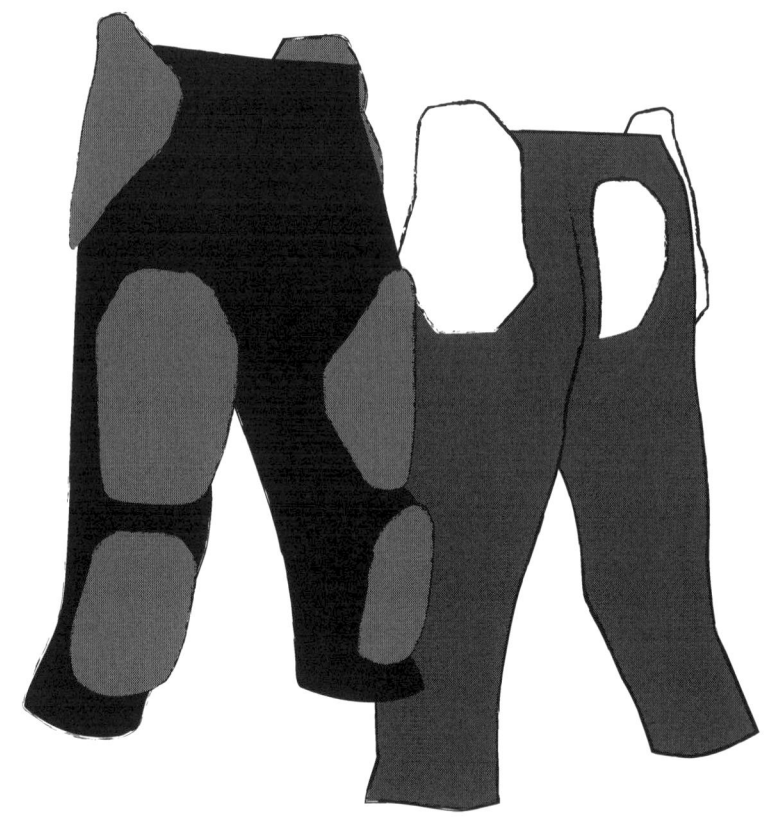

Figure 2.10 - Hip Pads, Thigh Pads, and Girdle

Knee Pads/Braces

Knee injuries are extremely common, and one of the most debilitating injuries a player can sustain. All too often we see ligaments being torn, bone contusions, and season-ending surgeries that are no match for even the greatest advancements in prevention. ACL (anterior cruciate ligament) tears are the most common injuries to the knees, followed by MCL (medial cruciate ligament) tears.

~ Fundamentals ~

I'm certainly no expert in medicine, but I can say from experience, that knees are nothing to be taken for granted. Several years ago I was walking into work wearing stilettos, when the cap of my heel got stuck in between a cement groove. I fell, causing a bone bruise/contusion to my femur, a torn MCL, and a crack in my patella. In that split second, I was strapped into a full leg brace for months, followed by rehabilitative therapy, and to this day, my knee is degenerating, all because of a shoe.

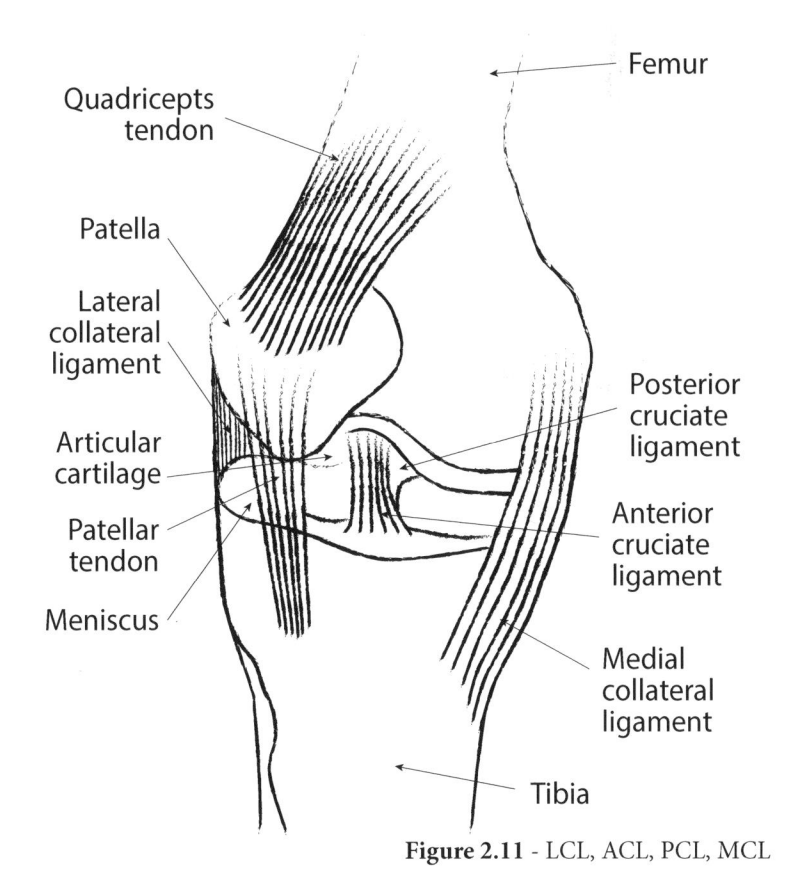

Figure 2.11 - LCL, ACL, PCL, MCL

Think of these ligaments as rubber bands, if you pull on them in awkward ways, or too hard, they're bound to snap. Football players cut, block, slant, tackle, and contort their beastly bodies in ways most of us can't even imagine (unless you were a test subject for the "50 Shades of Grey" film, of course). But prevention, preparation, and perhaps an occasional prayer, are the only things a person can rely on, and even then, they're walking a fine line.

Kneepads are truly a players' best bet, because they are designed to absorb the shock of impact – whether it's by another player, or the field they are playing on. Pads are made of either a gel, or foam, with a hard convex outer shell, and like all other components to the protective equipment, pads are placed into their respective pockets in football pants, or, there is the option to use a "sleeve."

Knee braces can either be used as another protective layer to combat violent hits, or to give knees that extra-added stability when recovering from pre-existing conditions. You will see them used on a myriad of positions, but mainly on offensive lineman, because when you're pinning up 6'6", 350-pound guys against 6'3", 260-pound linebackers, that extra protection in the pocket is imperative.

Cleats

Footwear is an important topic, and if you pay attention to the game, you will see a lot of things that simply don't make sense to us. For example, "Why do players wear different cleats on each foot?" and, "Why did kickers go bare foot?" It's an anomaly that women don't usually care about, but we probably should considering all the podiatric issues we bitch about.

Day after day, we strap up our Mile High Louboutin's, or stuff our tired feet into the cutest seasonal trends in footwear to tackle the world, but realistically, that's done at our leisure, so if we develop tendinitis, or other bone deformities, that's on us. Whereas, ballers don't have the option in selecting slippers or boat shoes, over their Nike Vapor Carbon Fly's on Game Days.

But really, why do football players wear different cleats on each foot? It's not that common, but it's mainly because different cleats offer different levels of comfort, protection, stability, traction, and grip. In the case of Pittsburgh Steelers' QB, Ben Roethlisberger during the 2010 NFL season, it had everything to do with his broken foot. Roethlisberger was forced to wear an oversized cleat, with two metal plates "fastened" to his ankle by athletic tape. More often than not, this will always relate back to a player with an injury, or that a dominant foot requires more traction or grip on a natural surface during inclement weather.

To answer why kickers went barefoot requires the understanding that they did some pretty weird shit back in the day, which we'll discuss in Chapter 3.

With all the bases on cleats pretty much covered, let's jump to an explanation of the injuries that can happen with, or without proper footwear, and why. *Turf Toe is explained below, and is the most common of injuries directly related to cleats. But Achilles injuries leave players susceptible to a wide range of injuries such as tendinitis, a rupture of the tendon (that occurs about two inches above the heel, causing severe pain, swelling, and other symptoms, that usually requires surgery), and your

~ Fundamentals ~

standard sprains and strains.

We need our feet to do just about everything, but explaining these injuries also relates back to us – women – in terms of what improper care, and what "flimsy" footwear can, and will, do to us. I know those "Buy One, Get a Pair Half Off" sales at sub-standard department stores sound like a good idea at the time, but athletes would never compromise quality over quantity when it comes to their feet, and you shouldn't either.

Vocabulary

- *Turf Toe*: the best way to explain this is that it's a sprain that occurs at the base of the big toe. This is mainly due to rigorous activity such as running, jumping, or other sudden movements such as cutting on artificial turf. This can – and will – sideline a player, because it causes limited mobility in the joint, along with a wide range of other symptoms, from inflammation, to severe pain. Several trainers I've talked to have said this is commonly caused by cleats that are "too flimsy", or don't offer enough support. Again, always contact a specialist when selecting footwear, or any other equipment.

Jock Straps v. Boxer Briefs

Now that I've taken you through a shitstorm of epic proportions regarding equipment and safety, it's time to settle the "what's he wearing" debate. Like I said before, asses, and us staring at them are just part of the game. Men have enough conversations regarding our boobs, so football should be payback, right? With that said, there's a certain fascination we have with male undergarments; this is why "boxers, or briefs" come as a standard question to ask, even on preliminary dates.

~ Fundamentals ~

Before getting into this, I want to say that the usage of a cup varies from leagues and coaches, but most Youth Leagues require them, as young athletes' bodies are still "developing."

A lot of critics say the jockstrap with added cup is the single most important piece of equipment a guy can wear, as they "cradle" testicles, and provide better support without the added layer of a compression short, which raises the temperature of their lower extremities.

This is all a matter of opinion to the guy who has to wear it, but it goes hand-in-hand with our never-ending bra debate. Sure a chiropractor might tell a woman who is more "endowed" that a mom bra (no offense) provides the best support, but a woman will wear what she wants to wear, and what she's most comfortable in.

Also, almost all the guys I know have said that they have a higher chance of taking a shot in the nuts from a friend acting like an asshole, than taking a foot to them on the playing field.

A high number of players from youth ball, up to the professional levels use jockstraps, but without the cup, and yes, there is a way to tell what he's wearing. If you see two thick lines through a players pants around the hips when he is down in his stance, or slightly hunched over at the line, he's wearing a jockstrap. If you see smooth lines, he's likely wearing compression shorts, which might be for added padding, or to omit pads in his pants, as previously discussed.

All things considered in terms of safety, athletes play at their own risk knowing the repercussions of their hobbies, but always remember that these injuries are common off the field, too. Every year, Leagues, Associations, Clubs, and everything in between, go above and beyond to enforce legislation to ensure player safety, even at the expense of changing the flow of the game. Your best bet is to always remain cognizant, that safety is the most important factor of this game – and any – and that no Super Bowl or Championship is worth paralyzation or ligament tears over because modern ball is "compromising history."

In conclusion to this section, you will hear about the "R.I.C.E." method a lot when it comes to sports medicine, and rehabilitation. It means "Rest, Ice, Compression, Elevate", and should always be an automatic response until a doctor can assess the injury. Whether you're screwing your knees up on stilettos, experiencing a sports-related injury, taking care of someone with one, or just acting recklessly, remember this basic acronym, and you should be ok. But always see a doctor as soon as possible, if not immediately.

4. Uniforms

If you've paid any attention to the ever-popular tributes to throwbacks around the League, and in College Football, you know that these are to pay homage to the forefathers of the game.

The detail, quality, and construction of football uniforms have improved exponentially since the early days. For starters, in the first football game ever between Rutgers and Princeton in 1869, players took the field in their casual street attire. History tells us that Princeton was the first team to present itself with organized team uniforms, which had a strikingly similar look to period baseball uniforms – even down to the shoe. Princeton also claims the title as having the oldest college mascot, the "Tigers", because their jerseys at the time resembled a prehistoric (Cincinnati) "Bengal'esque" color scheme, with orange striped trim and headwear.

It goes without question, the Ivy's revolutionized football in its entirety, and I swear at some point during this book I'll stop kissing their asses, but at some point, you'll also just have to join me in accepting the truth behind it.

Just so you can see how far uniforms have come in terms of quality and design, look up the 1895 Alabama Crimson Tide, and the swagged out 2013 Oregon Ducks.

It's been interesting to see how Oregon's uniforms have changed over the years, and much of this is attributed to their relationship with Nike – who operate out of Beaverton, Oregon, which is roughly 106 miles away from Eugene, Oregon, and home to the Ducks. Without "ruffling too many feathers", you can form your own opinion about that.

The sudden rise of Nike-powered uniforms (or "costumes", to some), is a widely scrutinized topic, because Oregon went from having a classic, clean, simplified uniform which resembled that if the Baylor Bears, and Green Bay Packers closets procreated, to having an entire arsenal of loud, distinct variations. In the 2000 season, Oregon introduced their highlighter yellow stripes, that have become synonymous with the Oregon brand, and since then, they've never ceased to amaze (or make one violently ill) with the design aspects. It's basically Bryant Park on ESPN, minus Lady Gaga, and is absolutely fascinating.

~ Fundamentals ~

Discussing all of the facets of uniform evolutions would require a separate book on football fashion, but to maintain our "simple" mantra, let's move onto the most basic elements involving uniforms themselves.

For starters, no other sport displays a players' number in more places, than in football, which are located – usually – on the chest, back, shoulders, and on many helmets. This is for a variety of reasons, but mainly so officiating crews, spectators, and commentators can differentiate between bodies with greater ease, and efficiency.

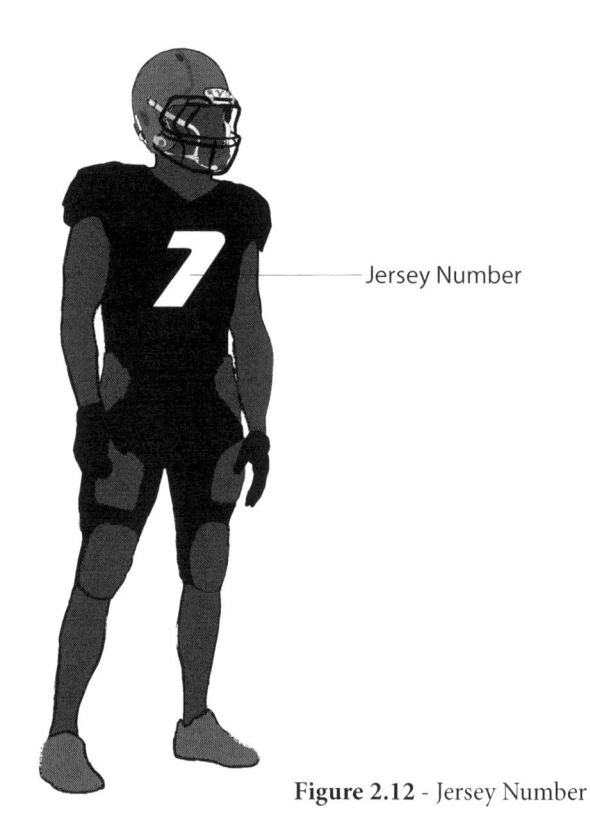

Jersey Number

Figure 2.12 - Jersey Number

~ Fundamentals ~

I'm sure most of you have figured out that numbers are designated to specific positions, but for the novice readers, uniform numbers range from 1-99, however, you will see multiples of the same numbers on a roster at any given time to accommodate a few factors.

For starters, former USC QB Matt Barkley and Safety T.J. McDonald both wore No. 7, and this is common, and as long as the like numbers maintain their separation by offense and defense, and no like numbers are on the field at the same time, it's fine.

I do want to point out that the most notable player who donned No. 99, was the legendary 2013 Hall of Fame Inductee, Warren Sapp. The Tampa Bay Buccaneers drafted Sapp out of the University of Miami in 1995, with the 12th overall pick in the first round. In his career, Sapp played in 198 games, registering 96.5 sacks, was a seven-time Pro Bowler, and Super Bowl Champion, (XXXVII) before retiring in 2007 with the Oakland Raiders. The most current badass to don the double-9's, is Houston Texans' DE J.J. Watt, who was voted by his peers as the No. 5 overall best player in the League in 2013, as well as leading the league with the most passes defended (blocked, or batted down), with 16 in 2012. If you hear analysts refer to Watt as the "Air Traffic Controller", that's why.

There is no ridiculous way to explain this, and yet despite being the most easily comprehensible factor of the game, people like to complicate it with the "high school v. college v. NFL" debate on stipulations and differences, so there's a chart breaking down the standard format on uniform numbers, on the following page.

~ Fundamentals ~

1. *Offense –*

    Quarterbacks: 1-19.

    Running Backs: 20-49.

    Wide Receivers: 10-19, 80-89.

    Tight Ends: 40-49, 80-89.

    Offensive Lineman (Centers, Guards, and Tackles): 50-79.

2. *Defense –*

    Linebackers: 50-59, 90-99.

    Defensive Linemen: 50-79, 90-99.

    Cornerbacks: 20-49.

    Safeties: 20-40

3. *Special Teams –*

    Punters and Kickers: 1-19

While the three different tiers of play have their own specific specialty rules, the chart above is as simplified as it's going to get. There are reasons why a kid can wear the same number from Pee Wee through the NFL, so learn this and eliminate everything else, but always be aware that there are loopholes and exceptions.

5. Personnel

Coaches, Team Personnel, Owners, and Management

It takes an army to manage, maintain, coach and mentor football players at any level, and any age. With that said, most coaches – at any level, really – deserve to be recognized for their role in helping mentor their athletes. It doesn't matter whether they're having problems at home, in school, or with life in general, they become father figures, and garner the trust of their players, so it's important that family remembers respect that bond.

Personnel and coaching staffs vary throughout the different levels of play and leagues, but that's primarily because of roster size, budget, and necessity, in terms of operations.

The Pee Wee, and Pop Warner-level "hands on deck", usually include the basics: a head coach, and a few other volunteers for specialty positions, plus a few more volunteers to provide the watermelon, and Capri Sun's (which better be cold, because I've heard some complain about this 20-years later). This level should be more about helping young kids develop social skills, leadership skills, the importance of respecting authority aside from their parents, and building character.

I've talked with a few guys about their first experiences with football, and many have said that from early ages, they were taught that winning was everything, and at any cost. That sends a bad message in the long run, because rarely do you hear about kids who were coached up to be assholes thriving both on, and off the field, plus having the ability to maintain that character (or their finances) past the pros, if they make it that far.

High school staffs are more complex because the coaching and mentoring kids receive there will decide whether they are going to play at the collegiate level, and what type of scholarships they'll be eligible for.

With that complexity, come stronger resumes and the ability to network the heck out of a community. This title requires extensive education in the sport, a degree (sometimes, even a masters if the institution requires it), simply because most coaches are also educators, a state-issued certification demonstrating knowledge, leadership, the understanding of safety and health, etc., followed by being in the right place, at the right time. While high school-level of play seems innocent, it can be extremely political.

Commonalities between levels of play:

- *Head Coach*
- *Assistants*
- *Offensive Coordinators*
- *Defensive Coordinators*
- *Running Back's Coaches*
- *Quarterbacks Coaches*
- *Receivers and Tight Ends Coaches*
- *Defensive Line Coaches*
- *Defensive Back's Coaches*
- *Offensive Line Coaches*
- *Special Teams Coaches*

Also, similarities include: refreshments personnel, audio/video staff who record games for analysis, and a highly charged and educated staff of athletic trainers on every sideline, prepared to handle any medical emergency or crisis.

The only real differences, are that extremely wealthy individuals who own NFL franchises have Front Office personnel, that include: presidents, chairmen, managers, national scouts/college scouts, and pro scouts, and their directors/coordinators (to scour the country every draft season for potential picks, and free agency potential), followed by combine scouts, security directors, statisticians, cheerleading coaches, and staff… an entire cabinet of positions directly related to how the team, facility, operations, and stadiums function, from customer service to legal, team nutritionists, orthopedic surgeons, doctors, video directors, equipment managers, rehabilitation specialists and their directors… the positions are endless, even down to the interns, sports analysts and reporters they employ.

While the college level offers the majority of what I just listed, the functions of their front office positions are managed by the Athletic Department, Sports Information Directors (SID), and Athletic Director, who are also in charge of making sure the NCAA Clearinghouse is alive and well, to clear student-athletes for participation, and for funding allocation, among other duties.

Many times you will read, or hear about issues arising from the Clearinghouse, but they usually have it together, so parents need not worry, as long as you are following procedures and seeking guidance, no matter how small the question or concern.

I want to add that college coaches, and NFL coaches (for the most part), have master's degrees, which are typically required for employment or candidacy. This is why so many former prolific college players whose careers go nowhere after they declare for the Draft, or run out of eligibility become coaches at junior colleges, or high schools, then move up from there. This also gives them an opportunity to apply as a Graduate Assistant at universities to understudy coaches, while working towards their masters. It should be noted that GA's are given a stipend to live off of, much like student-athletes themselves. Keep in mind that while this is the "usual" path, universities and teams will hire the best candidate, regardless of the educational resume.

6. Officiating

This section has dual parts: The Officiating Crew and Penalties. While both equally annoy us, a cold one at the concessions area works wonders to combat the blistering blows to our egos, especially if your team leads in penalties.

At the college level and in the NFL, there are *seven officiating crew members on the field at all times: The referee, umpire, head linesman, line judge, side judge, back judge, and field judge.

Other leagues and organizations are as follows: youth levels function with three officials, high school runs with four with the exception for varsity, who usually have five, along with arena, and semi-pro. Just remember that the higher you climb on the levels, the more rules and safety issues there are, so fortified enforcement is necessary.

~ Fundamentals ~

In the 2013 season, the Big 12 (CFB) began experimenting with an 8th official ("A", or Alternate), whose job is to spot the ball and increase efficiency on time between downs.

We've all wondered at some point, what the need for all these judges are, so here's a condensed breakdown:

- Referees: are the bosses. Plain and simple. They announce penalties and conduct all coin tossing procedures (start of game, and if a game goes into overtime). They are indicated by the "R's" on their uniforms, and are positioned behind the offensive side of the ball. They count players on the field (there should never be more than 11 on each side), observe quarterbacks, and all ball carriers specifically – including kickers.

- Umpires: are next in line, and are indicated by "U's". Their positions carry the greatest risks because they are situated behind the defensive side of the ball, and as we all know, the *Ray Lewis's of the football world can be scary people to be around at any given time. This increasing danger forced the NFL to reposition the Umpires next to the Referee's in the offensive backfield with the exception of *two-minute warnings in the first half, and during the last five minutes of each quarter in the second half, where they return to *Revis Island territory.

- Head Linesman: are positioned at the head of the line of scrimmage, are indicated by "H's", and are responsible for observing action near the sidelines. These officials are also in control of the chain gang (as discussed in the Scoring System section).

- Line Judges: are second to the Head Linesmen, and operate opposite of them. They are responsible for

~ Fundamentals ~

maintaining a secondary time for the game, enforcing, and calling fouls that occur before the ball is snapped, making sure kicks and punts are made from behind the line of scrimmage, and for all plays that occur 5-7 yards behind the line of scrimmage, like *laterals.

- Field Judges: count defensive players, operate downfield – on the same sideline as the line judge – and are responsible for calls involving running backs, wide receivers, and their defenders.

- Back Judges: also work with field judges to signal whether field goals are successful. They are indicated by a "B" or, "BJ", and have a similar responsibility for calling fouls for incomplete passes, pass interferences, illegal blocks, and for the same set of players. Back Judges are in control of the *backfield, and stand in the middle, deep behind the *secondary.

- Side Judges: are indicated by an "S", and are pretty much responsible for the same tasks as the field judges, back judges, and line judges, and to assist the Umpires during field goals – which is to stand behind the defense, and observe the offense. No further explanation is required.

~ Fundamentals ~

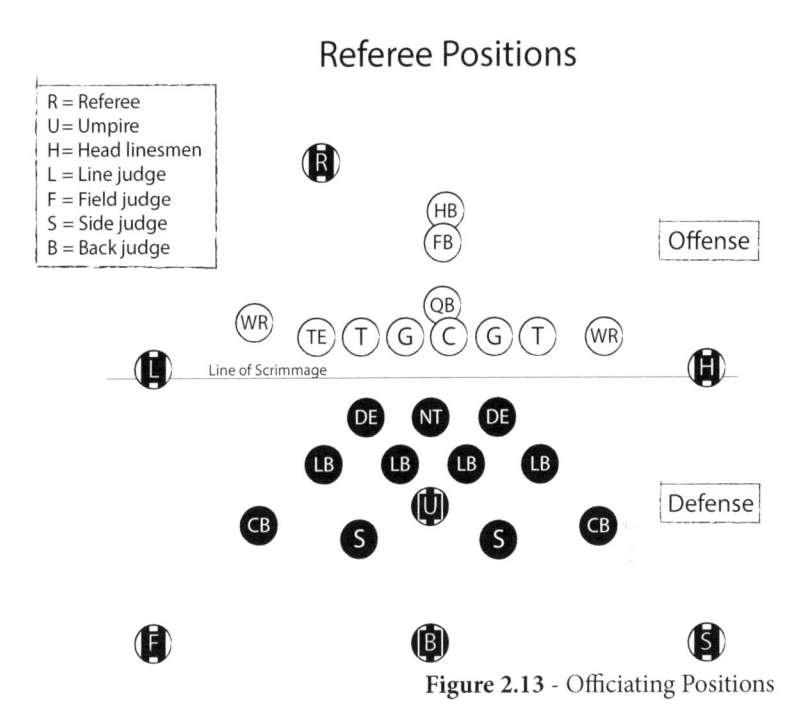

Referee Positions

R = Referee
U = Umpire
H = Head linesmen
L = Line judge
F = Field judge
S = Side judge
B = Back judge

Figure 2.13 - Officiating Positions

Vocabulary

- **Ray Lewis**: Was a Linebacker for the Baltimore Ravens for 17 seasons. During the October 14, 2012, 31-29 victory against the Dallas Cowboys, Lewis tore his triceps and was placed on Injured Reserve. He returned for the Playoffs and helped his team go to Super Bowl 47 in New Orleans, where the Ravens beat the San Francisco 49ers. Lewis retired immediately following. As of 2013, Lewis had won two Super Bowls (XXXVI, XLVII), registered 2,061-career tackles, 41.5 sacks, 18 forced fumbles, 31 interceptions, and three touchdowns. The 13-time Pro Bowler (one accolade out of a stellar Hall of Fame worthy list) was notorious for his ruthless intimidation, and for his ability to motivate his team, but he does have a questionable past.

Lewis was acquitted on charges of murder on January 31,

2000, after a Super Bowl XXXIV party when Jacinth Baker and Richard Lollar were stabbed to death as a result of a fight between Lewis, his entourage, and others. Lewis and friends, Joseph Sweeting and Reginald Oakley were indicted a few days after the murder, but murder charges against Lewis were dropped in exchange for his testimony against his friends, as no DNA from Lewis was found on the murder weapons (knives), and Lewis' white suit he was wearing that night was never found. Lewis was sentenced to 12 months of probation, charged with obstruction of justice, and fined $250,000 by the NFL – the heaviest fine ever issued by the league. In June 2000, Lewis' friends, Sweeting and Oakley were acquitted, and no other suspects were arrested or charged, leaving the case cold.

- **Two-Minute Warning**: is just that. A warning that is given at the end of the second, and fourth quarters, and regardless of play, the clock stops. This is only officially applied in the NFL, but college coaches receive a signal. Arena leagues implement a one-minute warning, whereas the Canadian Football League adheres to a three-minute. Dating back to the inception of the NFL, two-minute warnings were indicated by officials who kept time on their watches, to advise teams of how much time remained. In present day NFL, it's used as a strategy to motivate those last-minute drives, or as America has adopted – facetiously, or literally – Tebow Time.

- **The Backfield**: are the offensive players who line up behind the line of scrimmage, and behind the lineman or linebackers.

- **Revis Island**: named after Darelle Revis, who was a cornerback for the New York Jets (as of 2013, the Tampa Bay Buccaneers), and is used to describe his designated "stomping grounds" on the field, where wide receivers get their shit rocked. Usually. In September 2012 against the Miami Dolphins, Revis jumped over Miami center,

~ Fundamentals ~

Mike Pouncey trying to defend a screen pass, and in a non-contact, bizarre accident, went down with a torn ACL.

While our male counterparts tend to think that all those zebras on the field aren't necessary – and sometimes distracting – I can assure you that when your team is losing by three, with eight seconds left in regulation and offsides is called on the defense before the kick, which say… sails wide right, and PAST the uprights, you're going to want to buy a beer for the judge who called it, allowing your team the chance to kick again. Or, if your team was five yards away from a first down, they can accept the new set of downs. I've seen it happen all too often, and secretly your male counterparts have felt the same reaction.

I'm sure that some of you are asking, "WTF is a 'Zebra'?" Well, officials are often referred to as that, because of their uniforms.

The officials' uniform is common through any league and level, and while it oddly resembles prison attire, it significantly helps differentiate between bodies on the field. What *is* relatively easy to decode, are the penalties called based on the equipment officials use.

The first, and most apparent is the yellow flag we see thrown around during a game. This is to indicate that a foul has been committed, and the vicinity of where it lands, is where it's spotted. Also, officials usually carry multiple flags in the event of multiple fouls.

Bean bags are used to indicate points where possession of the ball has changed, for example: a fumble, where a punt is caught, or interceptions.

Down Indicators are elastic bracelets, with an elastic loop attached that can harness up to 4 fingers. These are used to help officials keep track of downs. Some officials use secondary Indicators to remind them of where the ball was spotted, by correlating hash marks on the field. For example, if a fumble occurs on the 23-yard line, the Indicator would be wrapped around the third finger.

Stopwatches are used so officials can keep track of game time, and to keep a comparable time for any disputes.

Sometimes you see officials taking notes on cards after significant events throughout the game; this is a tool used specifically for administrative purposes.

Then there's the whistle, which is used to indicate that the play is dead, or never began.

Penalties are quite possibly the most annoying topic when it comes to the game. Half the people watching think some of the calls are absolute bullshit, while the other half are sometimes too drunk to know what's going on. All they know, is that if they see their head coach throwing his headset to the ground in a fit of fiery rage, they respond with an arsenal of swear words that would make Rex Ryan look like a saint.

For reference purposes, these are the following calls we've already discussed:

- *False Start*
- *Encroachment*
- *Offsides*

~ Fundamentals ~

- *Neutral Zone Infraction*
- *Helmet-to-Helmet Hit*
- *Spearing*
- *Horse Collar*

More than likely, you're here to learn the basics of the sport, so here's a list of a few more penalties that I've seen get called often enough to be leave a memorable impact… even in moments of quixotic intoxication:

Vocabulary

- **Clip**: a clip is when an opponent is blocked across the legs, and from behind, resulting in a 15-yard penalty. Just imagine walking into a bar stool while your best friend drunkenly hits you from behind with a bear hug and leave it at that. It is very painful, I might add.

- **Illegal Shift**: is an infraction against the offense, where players move, or shift before the snap by changing positions and failing to reestablish, or reset and hold for at least a second after.

- **Pass Interference**: is when a player (usually on the defense, although offensive PI occurs) interferes with another players' ability to catch a fair pass. High school/college rules say that as long as the receiver is always in front of his defender, it's legal. PI at this level results in an automatic first down at the spot of the foul, and a 15-yard penalty. NFL rules say that the HS/CFB rule only applies for the first five yards, but results in an automatic first down. Offensive PI carries a 10-yard penalty.

- **Roughing the Passer**: when a player smacks into the quarterback after the ball has been released, resulting in a 15-yard penalty and an automatic first down. Late hits against the QB are anything that happens after he has released the ball.

- **Roughing the Kicker**: happens with a defensive player makes contact with any of the members on the kicking unit (Place Kicker, Punter, Holder), resulting in a 15-yard penalty. The only time this doesn't apply, is when the defensive player touches the ball *before* touching the kicker.

- **Delay of Game**: first let's go over the Play Clock, which lets teams and players know how much time they have to get the play off the ground. The CFL allows 20 seconds, whereas college, high school, and the NFL allow 25 seconds. Moving on, if the ball isn't snapped by the center (or longsnapper for a punt) within the time allotted, they get hit with a Delay of Game, which results in a five-yard penalty across the board.

- **Facemask**: is when an opponent grabs another players' facemask. It's a little more complex, however, as there are two different types: *Incidental*, which is when it's immediately released, and only results in a five-yarder. Then there is *flagrant*, which is when a player purposely grabs the facemask, and pulls his opponent down with it. This not only results in a 15-yarder, but it's also extremely dangerous.

- **Unsportsmanlike Conduct**: there really isn't another way to put this, other than when a player is acting like a douche. In my opinion, this is one of the worse penalties, because it's a personal foul that's strictly ego-centered. In the 2011 season, then, Tampa Bay Buccaneers head coach, Raheem Morris, sent defensive tackle Brian Price home for UC during their game against the Carolina Panthers. Why? Because getting flagged for taunting another player is selfish, and results in a 15-yard penalty. Regardless of whether a team is winning or losing the gridiron battle, there's no room for that. I will say,

~ Fundamentals ~

however, that Rule 13, Section 3, Article 1, Note 3 in the 2013 NFL rulebook, classifying home run swings, military salutes, and dancing as "unsportsmanlike conduct", is taking it way too far. In response to this in August 2013, the NFL stated that saluting was legal, as long as it's not directed at one player, specifically.

- *Illegal formation*: seven or more players are required to line up at the line of scrimmage for at least one second before the ball is snapped. If not, it results in a five-yarder.

- *Offensive Holding*: when a player on the offense uses his hands (mainly) to "hold" a defensive player, preventing him from advancing to the ball carrier. This results in a 10-yarder.

- *Defensive Holding*: when a defensive player holds or tackles an offensive player, who isn't the ball carrier. This results in a five-yard penalty and an automatic first down.

- *Illegal Crack Back*: is when an offensive player (usually a receiver or RB) who is outside the formation, goes in motion on the snap and runs to block an unsuspecting defensive tackle near the line of scrimmage. If contact is made above the waist, or five plus yards down field, it's legal. If it's below the waist, or on the LOS, it's illegal and a 15-yard penalty.

Officials Hand Signals

If I had explained every penalty throughout the various leagues, NCAA, high school, and lower, this book would easily be bulging at the seams with useless information. With that said, on the following page is a chart, with the basic hand signals correlating to the list of penalties explained above, and throughout this book.

~ Fundamentals ~

Clipping | Delay of Game | First Down | Touchdown | Holding

Inelligible Cut (block) | Inelligible Reciever | Illegal Motion | False Start | Illegal Use of the Hands

Intentional Grounding | Loss of Down | No Catch, Declined Penalty | Off Sides | Pass Interference

Personal Foul | Roughing the Kicker | Safety | Time In (start of clock) | Time Out (stoppage of clock)

Tripping | Touchback | Unsportsmanlike Conduct

Figure 2.14 - Hand Signals

page 63

7. The Season

As we move on to breaking down positions in the next chapter, I feel like now is the best time to bring up "The Season", and everything in between.

The truth about football, is that there never really is a defined offseason once you get past high school. As fans, we tend to overlook the business-related aspects because they don't directly impact our senses and emotions the way a touchdown scored at a game would. But truth be told, the 12-month calendar year is a non-stop work schedule and grind for athletes, coaches, staff, support members, and media.

Most cities and communities start celebrating the day before the game. For analysts, reporters, and crews, setting up begins a day before that, and the brains of the operation: coaches, staff, and players, begin the morning after the last one ended.

Whether it's the length of a youth season, or an NFL season, this is a non-stop operation. In this section, I'm going to explain what goes on from the locker room, to the field, press conferences, and everything in between, with a perspective to what the whole season looks like.

The struggle these athletes face is consistent at any level of play, so it's important to understand what they do, and respect it. In high school, an athlete is trying to get recruited, and it starts before his freshmen year. In college they're trying to make it to the NFL, and even if they make it to the NFL, there is absolutely zero guarantee they'll even have a career. After all, the acronym for NFL is, "Not For Long."

~ Fundamentals ~

With that said, I'll begin the work week, which starts immediately after the game. Standout players (even in high school) go through a gauntlet of reporters both on the field, and in the press conference breaking down highs and lows, and what needs to be improved for the following week. Players go home, and depending on how dedicated they are, or how rigorous the staff is, the team and coaches are back in the office the following morning, going over film and notes.

Players refer to the field, or facility as their "office", and it is.

For college ballers, the standard schedule is as follows: workouts, class, practice, more workouts, team meetings, class, and sleep. Wake up. Shower. Repeat. Somewhere in there, they get in food and a nap, and they do this on scholarships and stipends that are – in most cases – less sufficient than government assistance itself, that can average to around $4.50 an hour.

For professional ballers, this "struggle" comes with hefty monetary compensation, but even that isn't guaranteed. The Monday following a big win could include a four-year, $2,000,000 (and up) contract nullified for whatever reason, leaving him on the Free Agency wire for the other 31 teams to make a low-ball offer on.

Regarding Free Agents, let the truth be told that in most cases, they're on the market because they have flaws their former team deemed sufficient enough to release in the first place.

While us – as fans – tackle our weeks with normalcy, the guys that we celebrate, glorify, and idolize push through their uncertainty; combating fatigue, stress, financial burdens, grades, and more, just to pursue their aspirations, and for our entertainment.

~ Fundamentals ~

This same regimen goes on all week, followed by travel arrangements, the maintenance of eligibility, obtaining clearances for injuries, among other various factors for taking that field come game day.

For many NFL teams, and even some college teams, allocating four days, to an entire week for travel isn't uncommon. There are many wives and girlfriends of players and personnel, who will say that travel is one of the most stressful things about the game, on the business side.

For college athletes, this means registering for as many one day, three-hour, or online courses as possible, having tutors available at all hours of the day, and night, having to take exams early in some cases, and that isn't even fraction of the administrative issues that arise for them.

I hope that by now, a lot of you have increased your levels of respect for the demanding, and arduous things these guys have to go through, just to be able to "go to work" everyday. I wish I could tell you this was a matter of opinion, but it's a fact, and the same story I've been told by so many.

High school football doesn't require hotel stays, unless they are big games, or ones that require extensive travel. For example, Armwood High School from Tampa, Florida, at Bishop Gorman in Las Vegas, Nevada on August 27, 2011. Yes, games like this happen, and for the record, Armwood beat Gorman on a missed field goal, 20-17, but that win was voided as the result of a FHSSA (Florida High School Athletics Association) investigation, that found Armwood to be in residency violations.

This proves once again, that no player, at any level can get away with violating rules, and neither can their parents, so they'd be strongly advised against any, and all attempts. Remember, one violation directly impacts the entire team, coaches, school, and reputation, and could impact an athletes college recruiting, and potential future draft stock. Nothing goes without notice, and incidents won't disappear from their record, even if it's just a matter of public opinion.

College ball is a different story. The season (which runs a similar length as high school) starts in late August/early September, and goes until late November/early December. The calendar is 15 weeks, with one, or sometimes up to three weeks given throughout the schedule off, that is indicated as the "Bye" week.

For an example of scheduling, let's take a look at the Texas Tech Red Raiders 2012 schedule. They had an even number of six games at the Jones in Lubbock, and six games away. When scheduling, most conferences try and even out home, and away games, while taking in-conference, and non-conference games into negotiation and consideration, to make sure that schedules are balanced.

When taking stadiums into consideration, the Big 12 has some of the best scheduling in my opinion, because most teams get to play "At-Large" games at the Dallas Cowboys' AT&T Stadium in Arlington, Texas during their season. This is a great way to get players into a professional facility to see the arenas and stadiums they *could* call their "office" someday, especially one of that capacity, magnitude, and expense.

For comparison purposes, the SEC (Southeastern Conference), Pac-12, and various others implement this as well, but from discussions with the athletes themselves, modern, high-end stadiums for at-large games are more stimulating.

Several other factors are taken into consideration in regards to scheduling, including strength, travel, and healthy personnel. If a team is on the road for an entire month, it's obvious they're going to be worn down mentally, and physically.

Here's a breakdown of what the college season looks like:

1. Fall Camps start in early August, and last about two weeks;
2. The season begins in late August, and runs 15 calendar weeks;
3. Bowl Game Season goes from mid-December-up to a week-and-a-half after the new year;
4. Spring Ball practices start in late February (but if the team is invited to a late Bowl Game, it can be pushed forward a week);
5. Spring Ball games usually happen in mid, to late March, through April;
6. Practices and meetings through May, until finals;
7. Conditioning, training, 7-on-7's go the rest of the summer at the coaches and players' discretion, on top of summer camps, summer school, etc.

The NFL's regular season schedule is 17-weeks long and runs similarly to college, minus the academic issues. The biggest difference is that the team is distinctly run like a business, with no qualification-governing committees (NCAA) dictating eligibility. The only person who ever really sidelines a player – administratively – is the Commissioner, Roger Goodell, and this only happens when rules are severely broken. Otherwise, trainers and staff can sideline a player against his wishes in any event, but usually only when he's injured. In some cases, an athlete's pending legal proceedings will sideline the player, or get him cut entirely to avoid public backlash, or involvement.

I'm going to explain the NFL schedule the only way I know how, and from the perspective of the athletes themselves, because I've been given the opportunity to experience this through friends in the league, and I can tell you firsthand that it is brutal.

Say you're a college senior and you just played in your final bowl game. The feelings are overwhelming, and win or lose, the tears run down your face knowing this is the last time you will ever be on the same field with guys you grew to love like brothers. The realization that you are no longer an amateur, and about to make the biggest sacrificial decision of your young life and declare for the NFL Draft hits you, but just for that night, you want to celebrate, and let it all sink in.

In most cases, athletes will take up to a week after to decide on the person who will represent them as they move on to the next level. This isn't an easy decision. Most people take the agent process for granted, but the reality is, when that athlete signs his name on that contract, he is trusting whoever he just hired to represent him through several processes: from selecting the facility the athlete will be training at, endorsement deals, private workouts, salary negotiations, and more.

I want to note, however, that most athletes say they dislike having agents, and would fire them tomorrow if they could do the work themselves. It's relative to hair or nails for us; while our relationships with our stylists and techs aren't contractually based, you'd fire them in a second if they ruined your hair, right? And don't lie, if we could do our hair and nails ourselves at that level, we probably would.

The agent selection process happens fast, because time is of the essence. The second he signs, he starts shopping for the place he'll be training at over the next few months. Most of these training facilities offer everything from conference rooms, to press rooms, rehab, nutritionists… doctors even, so this selection process can be as grueling as picking an agent itself.

Once the facility is locked in, training begins. There are three possible senior bowls that top-prospects are invited to: The East/West Shrine Game, which has been played from San Francisco, CA to St. Petersburg, FL, the Senior Bowl held every year in Mobile, Alabama, or the NFLPA Bowl (formerly Texas v. The Nation Bowl [2007 – 2010] when it was in El Paso, TX and San Antonio, TX), that is currently played in Carson, California. These games are usually played at the end of January, with the Senior Bowl scheduled a week before the Super Bowl in February.

Every year, scouts and analysts break down, and dissect athletes to see where mechanics have been tweaked, but these guys are fresh out of college, and are being heavily evaluated on just several weeks of professional-level training. You might ask if that's fair or not, but a lot of these young athletes will be taking the starting positions for veterans eight months later, so it's important to sort out the quick learners to rank on draft boards.

When the exhibition games are over, players head back to their facilities to prepare for workouts. If the player received an invitation, he focuses on training for the exclusive NFL Scouting Combine that takes place at the end of February, and is held at Lucas Oil Stadium, in Indianapolis, Indiana – home of the Colts.

Usually after the Combine, players head back to their respective schools, or hometowns to prepare for Pro Days that happen all throughout the month of March, where private workouts are also scheduled, and can go right up to the eve of the Draft.

What's next? The NFL Draft, which is usually at the end of April, and held in prime time at the legendary Radio City Music Hall in New York City, New York. The 2014 NFL Draft will be on May 8-10, per the annual NFL Owners' meeting in 2013.

Immediately after the player is drafted, he usually flies out to his respective teams city for photo ops, press conferences, and the circus of "Welcome to (insert city here)" fanfare.

Players who go undrafted become Rookie Free Agents, where their agents negotiate workouts with teams, and players are monetarily compensated on a week-to-week basis in hopes of sticking a team and getting a contract.

In mid, to late May, players show up at their facilities for about three days for Organized Team Activities, which are designed to get rookies acclimated to their surroundings, coaches, etc., but are also provided to give league veterans opportunities to work on fundamentals, mechanics, or anything else that might need some attention before mini-camps.

A few weeks later, the players are all back for mini-camps that run through June. Towards the end of the month, Draft picks head over to a four-day event called the Rookie Symposium, which is designed to teach rookies everything from balancing their checkbooks, to investments, drugs, alcohol, fast women, and lectures on life from heavily qualified league brass. Following this, they have a few weeks off (where the dedicated still train) until the end of July, when they report back to their cities and start fall camps.

Training camps begin in late July, and run a few weeks. Then pre-season comes, which makes for an insanely chaotic month of August, and then BOOM, September 1 and the regular season hits, rosters are trimmed, and the journey to the Super Bowl begins. This, of course barring roster cuts, injuries, and tweaks throughout the 17 weeks before the Playoffs.

I know this was a lot to take in, but it's what these players go through. In fairness, I did warn you. More extensive explanations of the Combine, Pro Days, the Draft, and more will be further along in Chapter five.

Chapter Three
Positions

I wish this chapter could be skipped in its entirety, but it's obvious that a high number of women don't know what the different offensive, defensive, and special teams positions are, and what their jobs entail.

If you consider this a strong point in your football knowledge, then bypassing this chapter is obviously optional, but a little remedial reading never hurt. Just like quarterbacks have to throw passes over and over for muscle memory, our brains work the same way.

The Offense

The offensive positions are as follows:

1. Quarterback
2. Running Backs
3. Tight Ends
4. Wide Receivers (also called the Wideout)
5. Center
6. Guards (Left and Right)
7. Tackles (Left and Right)

~ Positions ~

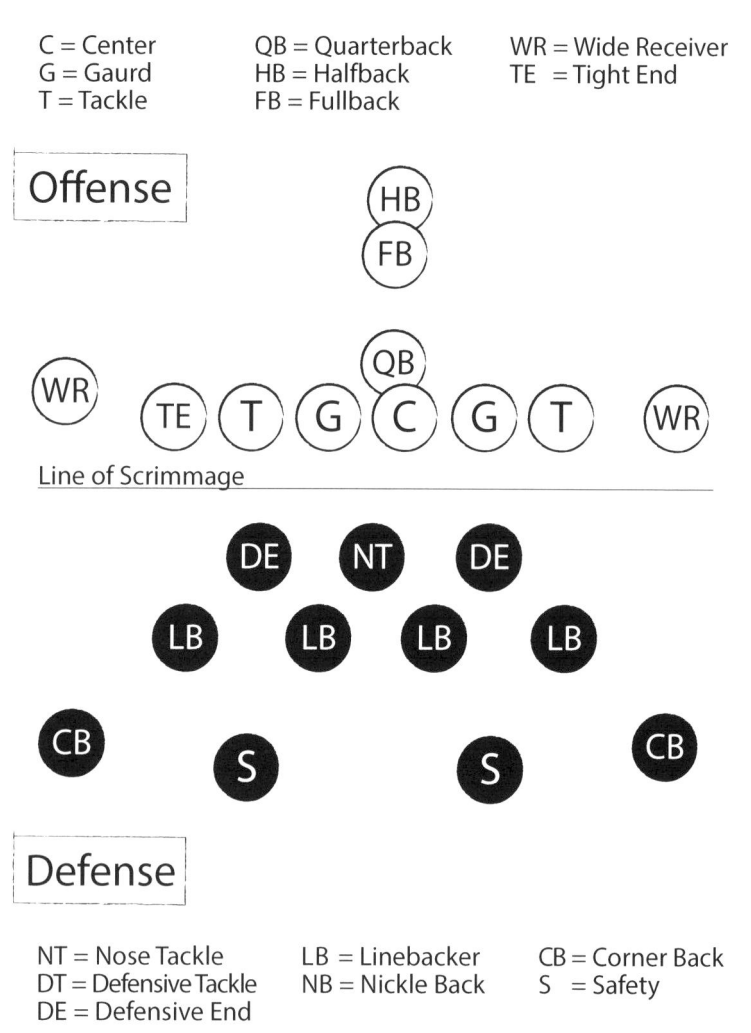

C = Center
G = Gaurd
T = Tackle

QB = Quarterback
HB = Halfback
FB = Fullback

WR = Wide Receiver
TE = Tight End

Offense

Line of Scrimmage

Defense

NT = Nose Tackle
DT = Defensive Tackle
DE = Defensive End

LB = Linebacker
NB = Nickle Back

CB = Corner Back
S = Safety

Figure 3.1 - Offensive & Defensive Sides of the Ball

The Breakdown

Let's start from the top with the Quarterback. From 2012 regular season NFL leader Peyton Manning (total QB rating of 84.1 -

page 74

~ Positions ~

Denver Broncos), to Braxton Miller (NCAA – Big 10: Ohio State Buckeyes), quarterbacks are the captains of any team, whose job description includes learning every play – both on offense and defense. They are the team ambassador for press conferences and interviews, before any of their teammates (even defensive captains), because they are in fact, the center and focal point of the team.

During the 2011 "offseason" when the NFL was in a massive labor dispute, and players were locked out, NFC-South, New Orleans Saints rainmaker Drew Brees lived up to his hype and organized voluntary workouts between him, and his teammates at various locations – most notably Tulane University in New Orleans. While players and coaches couldn't interact, or even receive playbooks, Brees did what any leader would have, and dedicated his summer to mobilizing his troops, and making a statement about his dedication to the organization. Subsequently, he eclipsed Miami Dolphin great, Dan Marino's single season passing record on December 26, 2011 against NFC South foe, the Atlanta Falcons, on a nine-yard pass to Darren Sproles for 5,087 yards (three-yards more than Marino in 1984), and is now the second highest paid quarterback in the league, under Green Bay Packers' Aaron Rodgers.

The offensive backfield, are the players who line up behind the offensive linemen.

The basic routine of the QB, is to stand directly behind the Center, read the defensive formation, project the play to the other ten soldiers on his side of the ball, call an audible (if necessary), and as soon as the ball is snapped, go with a few standard options:

~ Positions ~

1. Hand the ball off, or pass it on a *screen to a RB;

2. Hang in the pocket and check off any of his eligible receivers to pass the ball to;

3. Or, run like hell for yardage. The problem with quarterbacks who are notorious for the third option, is that defenses will read it, adjust, and make it their mission to go to Pound Town on a *blitz party.

QB's are the most widely scrutinized and judged position, and there are several things fans and analysts look for when determining if he's an elitist. This includes (but isn't limited to) how long he stays in the pocket, his release, his ability to check off receivers, and the ability to throw a beautiful spiral. A QB with size like a tight end is also important, so he can see over the line and read the defense. Also, God forbid he throws a pick, he can block in the backfield.

Of course, the ability to communicate with his players is a huge factor, and any player will tell you that how a QB projects his voice is everything, especially in a loud, unforgiving stadium. Fall back a few chapters to how crowd noise affected players at Quest Field in Seattle, Washington, and you'll understand why.

The Halfback, Tailback or Fullback IS A RUNNING BACK.

The job of the Fullback is to provide *pass protection for the QB, and block for the halfback. FB's are also used on short yardage passes. This position is also referred to as the tailback.

The Halfback lines up behind the QB, or to the side. Like the fullback, he acts as a blocker, and is used on short-yardage plays, but he's responsible for the majority of the carries, and is commonly used as an alternative back/option in case the receivers are covered, or backs are being blocked.

Simplified: Running Backs are part of the offensive backfield, and are the guys the QB hands the ball off to, or they are used as blockers. A few of the most popular RB's in modern day ball are Reggie Bush (Detroit Lions), Trent Richardson (Cleveland Browns), Silas Redd (transferred to the University of Southern California, by way of Penn State Sanctions), and top 2012 NCAA leading rusher, and Mountain West Conference record-setter, Stefphon Jefferson out of Nevada, who went undrafted in 2013. Let this be a clear indicator that no matter what records a player sets, or where he falls on a "leaders" board on ESPN, a Draft spot is NOT guaranteed.

Tight Ends have such a badass position because they get the best of both worlds: blocking (like an offensive lineman), and receiving (like a wideout). They're positioned on the line of scrimmage next to the left, and right tackles due to their size and ability to catch, and when you hear people discuss this position, they'll refer to it as a "hybrid" because they posses qualities of two job titles.

The most popular TE's in the NFL right now are Jason Witten (Dallas Cowboys, 6'6", 260 pounds), Jimmy Graham (New Orleans Saints 6'7", 265 pounds), and the infamous Rob Gronkowski (New England Patriots 6'6", 265 pounds).

The average height college recruiters look for is 6'3", so the stats I just listed should be a helpful metric for parents wondering where their kid needs to be. All that aside, TE's posses incredible speed considering their size, which is why I say that they get the best of both worlds.

~ Positions ~

Wide Receivers are lined up about a yard behind, and several feet to the left, or right of the TE's, and are responsible for long-yardage passes. When these passes are caught, it's referred to as a reception. The WR is typically the fastest, agile, most illusive, and acrobatic of all the positions throughout the board, so it should be easy to understand why some of the best highlights on game days come in the form of a wideout with leaping endzone receptions, because of these characteristics.

Their size typically ranges from 6'0"-6'3", and 200 to 230 pounds, with big hands so they can catch just about any ball.

The WR's performance is based on a number of factors, including how the QB throws the ball, how much of a spiral it has (a poorly thrown ball won't travel as far, or have the greatest accuracy), and how much coverage he has. If the QB throws a shitty ball, the WR has to make split second decisions like whether to cut across, which slows his momentum… and all while keeping his eyes on the ball. Even if the QB throws a perfect ball downfield, the reception is then based on how the WR is able to bust coverage, or avoid the tackle. The bottom line, is that you'll see wideouts go bat shit to make the play, whether it means smacking against walls seconds after the catch, doing flips, or Supermaning the ball inside the pylons on diving receptions to hit the six (score a touchdown) – they'll do whatever it takes.

In reference to cutting across the field, every time you watch analysis, the commentator will discuss differences between a player traveling "North and South", versus "East and West". Obviously the latter is what a player doesn't want to be doing, so hopefully this prevents a few blank stares if you ever ask what it means.

~ Positions ~

The success of WR's is difficult to predict, because their percentages are based on the number of receptions, versus the yards. For example, 18 receptions for 107-yards, means there was an average of 5.9-yards per reception, and less than the equivalent of a first down. The objective is to have lower receptions, with higher yardage.

Some noteworthy receivers are Chad Ochocinco/Johnson (Pro Bowler, 67 touchdowns since drafted in 2001), A.J. Green (Cincinnati Bengals, two-time Pro Bowler, with 18 TD's receiving for 2,407 yards since Drafted in 2011 out of Georgia), Justin Blackmon (5th selection in the 1st round of the 2012 NFL Draft by the Jacksonville Jaguars, from Oklahoma State) and Kenny Stills, who averaged roughly 13 yards per reception in his career at Oklahoma, and is sure to turn some heads this season in the NFL with the New Orleans Saints.

Now that the backfield positions have been addressed, it's time to explain the spine of the offense: The Offensive Linemen. The Center, Guards, and Tackles are my favorites because they're notoriously large, teddy bear-like in stature, protective, and extremely intelligent. It goes without question that you want an athlete who not only can block the shit out of defenders for the QB, and RB's, but also make quick, and smart decisions while doing so. Offensive Linemen – on average – score the highest on the Wonderlic, which is a 12-minute, 50-question NFL exam used to test a players' cognition and problem solving abilities.

Offensive Linemen are typically 6'5"+, 300 plus pounds, with big hands, incredible strength, the ability to balance their massive bodies in a *three-point stance, and maintain quick feet while doing so, to pop up and block.

~ Positions ~

The Center stands in front of the QB, and has the role of snapping the ball to him. Whenever you hear situations among teams where they have QB battles, this becomes a headache for the center because as previously discussed, the QB's play calling and voice projection gets embedded into the memory of the center, and can be problematic when listening for the snap count through thick crowd noise. This is also why QB's are seen stomping their feet to give a visual snap.

Guards and Tackles have parallel job descriptions, where they create a *"pocket" to protect the QB by blocking defenders, providing pass protection, and by creating holes for RB's. The only differences really, are where they are situated and provide protection: inside, and outside.

O-linemen can also be versatile as eligible receivers, but the officials have to be made aware of this personnel change, and at that point, he lines up behind the line of scrimmage similar to where the TE would. This is easy to spot, if you know what the basic offensive formations look like.

When a lineman has possession of the football, I call it a "Big Boy Giddy-up", and I'd have to say that one the best recollections of this in recent history happened in 2011 by San Francisco 49ers' LT Joe Staley against the Browns in Week 8. Former SF QB Alex Smith ran a *play-action fake that left Staley – who had lined up as a TE – open downfield where he caught his first career reception, and got a first down.

I know that as women, we're initially going to be more attracted to the QB's, WR's, RB's, TE's… shit, even the kickers, but always bear in mind that the OL is the anchor that holds the offense

~ Positions ~

together. If their 1,600-1,800 pound wall of twisted steel and sex appeal collapses, so does the pocket, and likely some ligament on the QB. I challenge you to shift your focus on the OL at some point this season, to see what I'm talking about.

Vocabulary

- **Screen**: a short, forward pass to a RB when the defense has blitzed the QB, allowing the OL to block for the RB. This is a tactical play, where the defense is allowed to blitz, and rush the QB. Again, if the defense hits the QB after the ball is released, it's a late hit, which results in 15-yards and an automatic first down.

- **Blitz**: this is when the defense – specifically the linebackers, or defensive backs – charge into the offensive backfield with an objective to sack the QB, or rush the pass. It's designed to hurry the pass.

- **Pass Protection**: when the offense blocks for the QB to protect him on passing plays.

- **Red Zone**: this isn't just an Old Spice Men's deodorant; it's an imaginary line (or red-shaded, and provided by Verizon – usually – if you're watching from home) that marks the 20-yard line, to the goal line. Referring back to Tebow, this is where the majority of his scoring magic happens.

- **Pocket**: this is the 1,600-1,800 pound wall of O-Linemen body mass that protects the QB. Think of the QB as a Christian Louboutin Daffodil pump; the ones encrusted in Swarovski crystals. When they're in the dust bag, they have the greatest protection, so think of that as the OL, or pocket. Whenever those expensive red bottoms (or teal, which can be custom ordered at the flagship store) come out of the dust bag, however, they are subject to wear, tear, and the loss of crystals. The QB loses value in

~ Positions ~

a much similar way. A Daffodil without crystals, is about as alluring as a QB with a jacked up knee.

- *Play Action*: when a QB fakes a handoff to a RB, then drops back, and fires it when he sees his eligible receiver open downfield.

- *3-Point Stance*: a formation which all of their body weight is evenly distributed to their feet, and one hand. They are precisely balanced, yet OL can pop out of the position to block oncoming defenders in a split second. I actually recommend each, and every one of you to drop down into this formation and see if you can balance your body weight. It's a hard stance to maintain, but will show your level of athleticism compared to the "big guys."

- *Lateral*: is when the ball is pitched (thrown) backwards and laterally (east/west) to another player.

Offensive Plays

Most of us have seen, or held an amateur-level playbook, but they hardly measure up to the cinder block weight of a professional one, which is partially why most NFL Franchises have started issuing iPads, with the books downloaded.

Here are a few of the offensive basics:

- *Spread Offense:* is when the QB runs out of the *shotgun, with multiple (3, 4, or 5) WR's spread horizontally to create and open vertical seams (along with offensive linemen, in some cases), forcing the defense to "spread" itself out thin. The spread is used at every level, in every league, and is pretty successful. Washington State head coach Mike Leach ran the spread (along with the Air Raid) during his tenure at Texas Tech, and it quickly

~ Positions ~

became one of the top offenses in the country.

- *Air Raid*: (an extension of the *Spread*) was made popular by Hal Mumme, Mike Leach and Sonny Dykes, and heavily utilizes wide receivers. The QB lines up out of the shotgun, with two inside (slot) and two outside receivers (plus one running back, typically). The Air Raid is usually no-huddle (or hurry-up), and gives the QB flexibility to assess the defense and audible a run play depending on how the defense is adjusted. Most offenses that install the Air Raid, pass the football on up to 75 percent of calls during a season. The beauty of the air raid is that defenses will tire faster, allowing for greater plays on offense. The offensive linemen are spread out a little farther to widen passing lanes and make DE's run farther to get around the OT's for a sack, despite opening up easier blitz lanes. But the QB usually just throws a short pass or screen to avoid the blitz. There are several different installations and packages, but that's the basic explanation.

- *West Coast Offense*: put simply, means it's an offensive scheme designed for passing plays, that are usually short, and intermediate yardage passes, intended to open up routes and create better control of the ball. The main utility of the West Coast Offense is to create mismatches between offensive, and defensive players, by overwhelming the defense with receivers. USC is a team that runs this effectively, along with most teams who are heavy on WR's. The problems are that defenders are so fast now, that it doesn't work the way it used to when "The Genius", Bill Walsh invented it. Walsh was the head coach of the San Francisco 49ers from 1979-1988, where he won six division titles, three NFC Championships, three Super Bowl's (XVI, XIX, and XXIII), named NFL's Coach of the Year in 1981, and 1984, and was inducted into the Pro Football Hall of Fame in 1993. After battling leukemia since 2004, Walsh passed away on July 30, 2007 in California, at age 75.

~ Positions ~

- ***Pro-Style Offense***: is exactly that. Professional leagues employ only the best because they've demonstrated they're elitists, with the ability to *run block, *pass block, and run crisp *routes with marginal room for question or error. If you watch pre-draft analysis, you will often hear seasoned retired veterans discussing this as "intangible" for some prospects, because they strongly believe that the player can't adapt. To be as transparent as possible, it's a broad term to describe all the complexities utilized in professional-level offensive formations, and positions.

- ***I-Formation***: is the contrast to the West Coast Offense and is designed for running plays. TE's and receivers are used for blocking in this situation, with the tailback lining up around seven-yards behind the line of scrimmage to survey the defense, and is used as a blocker.

- ***Pistol***: (another extension of the *Spread*) was developed by University of Nevada head coach Chris Ault (retired in 2012, and is currently a consultant for the Kansas City Chiefs) in 2005, as a way to add a running assault to the spread. It's pretty much when a quarterback lines up about a yard closer (and four yards behind the center) to the line of scrimmage, so he can read the defense more efficiently, get the ball to the RB (who is about three yards behind the QB) faster, and read the field more clearly. This generally allows a threatening versatility, where the QB decides to hand off, make a pass downfield, or maintain possession and run it in himself, called the Read Option. Everyone from UCLA, Oklahoma, Florida, the 49ers, to the Pittsburgh Steelers have used this, or an adaptation in some way or another.

- ***Wildcat Offense***: Is when the RB lines up under center, takes the snap, and has the option of running with the ball, or passing it. Some QB's line up as TE's or WR's during this formation – or package – which makes it difficult to defend.

~ Positions ~

- *Bootleg*: is when a QB pretends to hand the ball off, then runs with it in the opposite direction - behind the line of scrimmage - to deflect defenders. He has the option to pass it, or run it in himself.
- *Naked Bootleg*: Is the same as the bootleg, but the QB is on a solo mission, without blockers.

Based on observations during games, here's a list of offensive vocabulary, that you will need to know:

Vocabulary

- *Flea Flicker*: when the QB hands the ball to a RB, who pitches the ball backwards *and* laterally (east/west), before the line of scrimmage to the QB. It's a trick play because the defense then has to backpedal to the QB, and by that time, he's likely already hit a receiver downfield.

- *Shotgun*: when the QB takes the snap from several yards behind the center. This gives him more time to find open receivers downfield.

- *Run Block*: is when members of the offense "bull rush" the defense, creating holes for the RB's on running plays.

- *Pass Block*: is when the o-line creates a wall to push defenders back, or stop them so the QB can pass the ball.

- *Routes*: in themselves are practically buffet tables in a playbook, but they're designed for WR's to run and get open for a pass. This includes (but is certainly not limited to) a wheel route (outer edge of field, versus on the inside), post route (kind of lined up with the field goal posts), and a slant route (receiver runs straight up the field, then cuts at a 45 degree angle).

page 85

~ Positions ~

- *Triple (Option)*: you will hear this a lot during games, but all it means is the QB is pulling out all the tricks. It includes checking off WR's, running with the ball, handoffs to backs, and more. This happens when the QB sees a defender (usually a defensive end) running at him, he'll likely hand it off or pitch it. If he sees defenders all over the backs or receivers, he keeps it, called: Option Keeper. The Triple Option varies with offensive formations.

- *Multiple Receiver Set*: is a component in the Spread, which is designed as a "run first" offense. It just means that there are multiple WR's.

- *"Late On His Reads"*: means that a QB is hesitant, and literally late reading his personnel to get the ball off.

- *Gap Assignments - A Gap*: is the Space separating the Center and Guards.

- *Gap Assignments - B Gap*: is the space separating the Guards and Tackles.

- *Gap Assignments - C Gap*: is the space separating the Tackles and Tight Ends.

~ Positions ~

The Defense

The defensive positions are as follows:

1. *Linemen*

    Defensive Tackle

    Defensive Nose

    Defensive End

2. *Linebacker*

    Middle Linebacker (MIKE)

    Strong Side Linebacker

    Weak Side Linebacker

3. *Defensive Back*

    Safety

    Strong Safety

    Free Safety

    Cornerback

Visual Aid: See figure 2.15

Linemen include the Defensive Tackle, Nose Tackle, and Defensive Ends, who line up on the line of scrimmage, across from the offensive linemen. Their objective is pretty obvious: to stop forward progress of the football, sack the QB, and create turnovers.

There's an expression that says, "The best defense is the one on the bench", and while this might be true to some, the best defenses are fast, agile, and will stop at nothing to take the ball carrier down. Obviously this doesn't pan out the way defensive coordinators envision at times, but if a defense can even force a *three-and-out on their own 40-yard line, sure time has been shaved off the clock allowing for the forward movement of 60-yards, but it sure beats allowing points.

Low scoring games irritate people; I used to be one of them, until I realized the game then becomes a battle over who has the best defense. Looking back at the 2011 season, when LSU (Louisiana State University) took on SEC rivals Alabama on November 5, 2011 (who they'd face again in the 2011 National Championship), 60 minutes elapsed, and a combined total of only 12 points were scored by the nations No. 1, and No. 2 teams. TWELVE POINTS. Why? Stellar defenses who only allowed field goals, and another field goal in overtime by LSU to win it. When situations like this arise, it's time to put the "I only get excited when my team scores" mentality in the garbage, and invent drinking games to celebrate *sacks, tackles for loss, or when a pocket is dismantled.

The Breakdown

Defensive Tackles line up on the interior of the line, and their objective is to apply pressure up the gut to stop passing plays, and also contain RB's on running plays. The most notorious DT's in history are Warren Sapp (whom I've already discussed), and Cortez Kennedy of the Seattle Seahawks, who was an eight-time Pro Bowler, and 2012 NFL Hall of Fame Inductee.

~ Positions ~

Nose Tackles line up directly between the DT's, and across from the center. Their main objective is to stop the run, and occupy the offensive linemen.

Defensive Ends line up at the *end* of the defensive line. Duh. Their job is to contain the running game (RB's) so they don't have to chase them down, or rush the QB on passing plays. There are two DE's to reduce difficulty when swooping in on their targets. When you see DE's rushing the quarterbacks, it will be done in a number of ways, but mainly by batting the football down, or sacking the QB. Now, keep in mind, if the ball is batted down to force a fumble and it's recovered by the defense, they *can* advance the ball until they're tackled, forced out of bounds, or score, BUT their knees or elbows CAN NOT touch the ground. Because of that "swoop" function, DE's have to be fast, despite averaging between 240-260 pounds.

Linebackers form the first line of penetration for the defense behind the Tackles and Ends. LB's are broken down by: Middle Linebackers (MLB'S, or "MIKE"), Strong Side LB's ("SAM"), and Weak Side LB's ("WILL"). All three are assigned specific duties, such as protecting the run, and pass protection. They all weight around 250 pounds, they're all fast, and they're all certifiably bat shit insane.

"As a pass rusher, how fast can I get from point A, to point B?"
- Denver Broncos OLB, Von Miller.

One of the most popular LB's of all time is Dick Butkus, who was Drafted in the first round of the 1965 NFL Draft by the Chicago Bears, out of the University of Illinois. In his eight years with Chicago, Butkus put up quite a resume by becoming an eight-

~ Positions ~

time Pro Bowler, registering 1,020 tackles, 22 *interceptions, and was inducted into the NFL Hall Of Fame in 1979. He also has an award named after him: The Butkus Award, which was instituted in 1985. This is one of the nation's highest honors, and is awarded to the top linebackers in high school, college, and the pros every year. To clarify any grey area in that explanation, that's one award, three different levels, with three different winners.

MLB's (commonly called the "MIKE") secure their defense, call defensive audibles, and make sure all the players are set. When the play is in motion, his job is to stay on top of the ball during running plays and make the tackle, or assist in every way possible. For passing plays, he covers any backs that might option as receivers.

The objective of the Strong Side Linebacker is to cover and isolate TE's. So, basically do whatever necessary (and legal), to prevent him from catching a pass. And if he does, a painful tackle likely accompanies it.

Defensive Backs are members of the defensive backfield, who create the second line of protection behind the linebackers. This position – called the secondary – includes two Safeties, and two Cornerbacks, who's job is to provide protection on running plays, and defend passes by covering WR's.

Safeties line up farthest from the line of scrimmage, and behind the CB's. They are mainly designated to protect the outside and help CB's with pass coverage – specifically WR's. By definition, there are two types: Strong Safety, and Free Safety. SS's are the larger of the two, line up a little closer to the LOS than the FS, and help by stopping RB's if they get into the backfield. FS's fall back and gauge their moves by wherever the ball goes. They're a little smaller, but stealthily quick. The commonality between the two, are they both make tackles, and they hurt like hell because of the high rate of speed at which they attack.

There's a defensive scheme called "Cover 2", which simply put, is when the field is divided in half with each safety deep, covering his respective side, ready to throw down when his airspace is violated. The different variations of coverage are listed below. "Cover 3 Zone" is when three defensive backs (two CB's and one Safety) occupy their designated 1/3 of the defensive backfield. It's intended to reduce big plays downfield.

When most analysts think of Safeties, their minds automatically want to shift to Troy Polamalu of the Pittsburgh Steelers, and Ed Reed of the Houston Texans – who spent his entire career (2002-2012) with the Baltimore Ravens before becoming a free agent in 2013, when he signed with the Texans.

Aside from being a first round Draft pick in 2003, Polamalu – a Strong Safety – has quite the credentials to put him at the top spot. As of the 2012 season, his stat lines were 640 tackles, 10 registered sacks, and 30 interceptions. As stated previously, defensive players typically don't get reps with QB's, so this shows how fast and efficient the 31 year old, seven-time Pro Bowler, and 2010 AP (Associated Press) Defensive Player of the Year is.

Ed Reed is an absolute beast, but if you ever get to see him on any NFL Films, his personality is above the bar. His 5'11", 200-pound frame is the ideal stature for his Free Safety position, and like Polamalu, Reed was a first rounder, but in 2002. As of the 2012 season, Reed had registered 605 tackles, 11 forced fumbles, 13 touchdowns, and 61 interceptions, which he returned for 1,541-yards. He holds an NFL record of the longest interception return (for a TD), that happened on November 23, 2008, when he intercepted Philadelphia Eagles QB Kevin Kolb halfway through the fourth quarter, and ran it in 108-yards for the six.

Cornerbacks typically range around 6'0", 200 pounds and are ridiculously fast. Imagine running 40-yards in 4.45 seconds… that's how fast. The interesting thing about this statistic, is anything more than 4.45, and the CB is considered average, and he really becomes just another name on a piece of paper at that point.

CB's are wherever the WR's are, to intercept the passes, bat balls down, or push wideouts out of bounds. Because of their size, they typically won't engage in a confrontation where a tackle needs to be made, but will do just about everything else to break up the pass. CB's have either no time, or very little time practicing with QB's, so they intercept very few passes successfully. Simply put, if they were supposed to be badass receivers, they'd be playing on the other side of the ball.

To simplify what I just said, always remember that the guys on the line up front, are to cover the run game, whereas the guys in the back (field) cover the passing game, and receivers.

Vocabulary

- ***Three and Out***: when the offense is forced to punt on fourth down, because they can't get a first down in the first three plays of a particular drive.

- ***Sack***: is when the quarterback gets taken down when trying to throw a pass, behind the line of scrimmage.

- ***Interception***: when a member of the opposite team catches the ball during a forward pass.

- ***Pick***: is the same as an interception, however, when this happens it's referred to as "... he was picked off."

- ***Pick 6***: is the same as a Pick, except it's taken in for a touchdown; hence: 6.

There are many different variations of defensive schemes and plays, but here is a list of a few definitions based on popularity, and usage in football broadcasts:

- ***4-3 Defense***: when there are four linemen, and three linebackers.

- ***3-4 Defense***: when there are three linemen, and four linebackers.

- ***46 Defense (pronounced forty-six)***: is a 4-3 Defense created by Buddy Ryan (former NFL coach, and Bears defensive coordinator from '78-'85), and made popular by the Chicago Bears (when they beat the Patriots 46-10) during Super Bowl XX, on January 26, 1986. It involves a lot of shifting, but pretty much means when the linebackers shift to the offenses weak side, with the DB's (two CB's and one SS) crowding the line of scrimmage. The free safety hangs in the backfield, as usual.

- ***Cover 2***: when both Safeties cover their half of an (imaginary) split backfield.

~ Positions ~

- **Cover 3**: when two Cornerbacks and one Safety occupy their respective 1/3 of the defensive backfield.

- **Tampa 2**: is a defensive strategy adopted and made popular by the Tampa Bay Buccaneers during the Tony Dungy coaching era. To execute this properly, Middle Linebackers drop back, creating a Cover 3 in the backfield to provide better coverage on deep routes. Players are assigned to protect their respective gaps, tackle, and hustle.

- **Man-To-Man Coverage**: is when each member of the defense is assigned to individually cover each player on the offense.

- **Zone Coverage**: when defensive players are assigned to cover specific parts on the field – mainly DB's and LB's.

- **Safety Blitz**: an all out assault by both the strong safety, and free safety to hit the shit out of the QB, before he throws a pass.

- **Secondary**: this is the defensive backfield, and comprised of two Safeties, and two Cornerbacks.

- **Nickel**: this is a play strategically designed to stop the pass, and is when a fifth DB replaces a linebacker. Again, DB's are in the defensive backfield covering WR's, typically. This addition to the backfield is called The Nickel Back.

- **Dime**: this is the same as the Nickel, except that two DB's are brought into the backfield, replacing two LB's. This is to increase personnel on desperate offensive situations, to fortify pass protection. These additions to the backfield are called Dime Backs, because two nickels equal a dime.

~ Positions ~

Special Teams

Special Teams' positions are as follows:

1. Place Kicker
2. Punter
3. Holder
4. Kick Returner
5. Long Snapper
6. Punt Returner

Punt formation

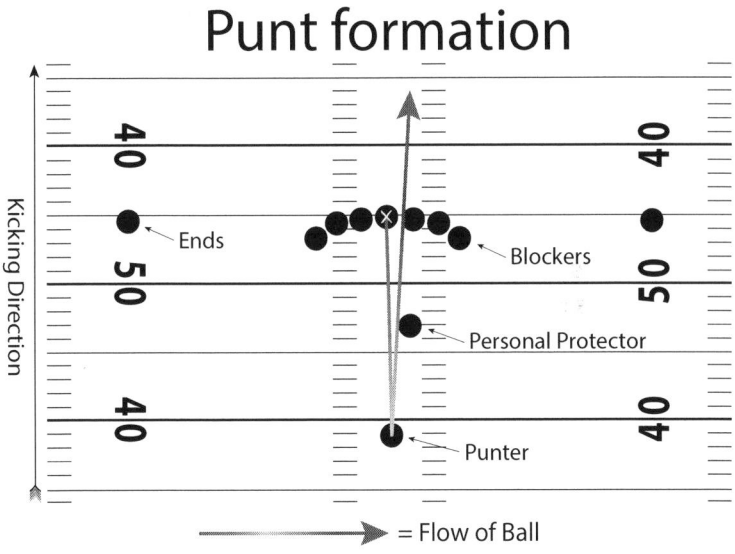

Figure 3.2 - Punt Formation

~ Positions ~

Field Goal Formation

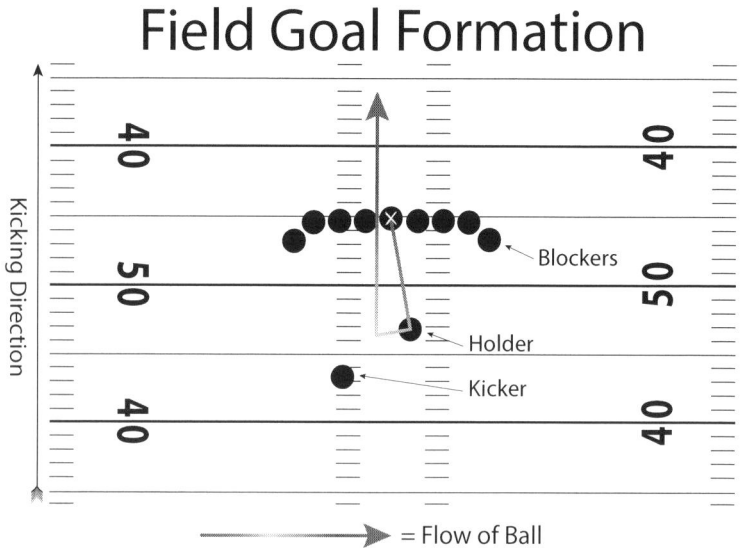

Figure 3.3 - Field Goal Formation

With the exception of an onside kick, the two formations that Special Teams assume when they're on the field are depicted on the previous page.

There's a huge misconception regarding the athletic ability these positions entail, because the majority of our focus is on the kicker. Special Teams personnel are made up of the best players from various positions on both sides of the ball. Positions ranging from the quarterbacks, middle linebackers, offensive linemen, cornerbacks, and more account for ST's, for a number of reasons. This is mainly because teams need players who have the ability to jump in front of kickers, jump up to deflect the football from up top if that fails, block, and run like an Olympic sprinter if there's a fumble and it's recovered by the defense. Also, if the kicking team fakes a field goal, or has a botched snap, a quarterback is on-hand to attempt a first down, or convert;

although, many times the kicker, or holder themselves assume this task.

Special Teams personnel, and their necessity have changed so much over the years, but none as great as the kicker itself. Most of these guys have crazy or interesting stories, but I pulled three of them from complete opposite sides of the spectrum to expand your history on the position, and add ammo to your growing arsenal of knowledge-fueled comebacks.

The first on this list is Antoni "Toni" Fritsch, who went from being a soccer player in Austria, to a Dallas Cowboy.

Fritsch had an awesome soccer career, and was known for his quick and accurate feet. In 1971, Dallas Cowboys' head coach Tom Landry was in the market for a kicker who possessed those traits, so he headed across the pond to poach a soccer player.

On Landry's first day in Vienna, he tried out Fritsch and signed him immediately. Fritsch – who barely spoke any English at the time – ended up playing for the Cowboys (1971-1975), the San Diego Chargers (1976), the Houston Oilers (now, the Tennessee Titans) from 1977-1981, and made his final NFL stop in 1982 with the New Orleans Saints.

In Fritsch's 11-year NFL career, he played in 125 games, scoring a total of 758 points, and helped lead the Dallas Cowboys to a Super Bowl victory against the Miami Dolphins on January 16, 1972 at Tulane University in New Orleans, LA.

The second of these badasses is Tom Dempsey. What makes Dempsey exemplary, is that he played under special needs circumstances; he was born without fingers on his right hand,

~ Positions ~

and toes on his right foot. Because of this, Dempsey wore a special shoe that was square-shaped at the front. Obviously controversy was focused on this situation, as players said his special needs footwear gave him an unfair advantage because he kicked straight on (as opposed to soccer style). Considering most kickers do not, in fact, kick "dead on", they would beg to differ. What I can say is that his skill solidified a decade of roster spots, and a Pro Bowl for him.

Hands down, the best account of Dempsey's professional career was on November 8, 1970 (again, at Tulane University), when the Saints were taking on the Detroit Lions. Dempsey booted a 63-yard field goal with two seconds left in regulation, to put them up 19-17 over the Lions. That's close to 3/4 of a football field, and a record that still stands to this day.

I'm going to start the final guy off, by asking if you've ever kicked a ball as hard as you could… barefoot? If your answer is yes, then you're just as much of a crazy ass as Tony Franklin. If you're from Aggieland (Texas A&M), you probably already know who he is, because he's a record setting, barefoot kicking, Texan.

Franklin was an All-Star kicker throughout his career, and subsequently got drafted in 1979 by the Philadelphia Eagles in the third round, with the 74th pick. Kickers never get drafted! I wish I was joking, but if you ever hear a kickers name get called, analysts and spectators exalt in a tidal wave of "WTF!" In his nine years in the league, Franklin played for the Eagles (1979-1983), the New England Patriots (1984-1987), and concluded his career in Miami, in 1988.

So what happened to barefoot kickers? I'm going to go on a limb here and say they stopped, because it hurt. I actually did quite a bit of research on this, and Rule 5, Article 3, Part (g) in the NFL Rule Book states, "Barefoot punters and placekickers may omit the stocking of the kicking foot in preparation for and during kicking plays." There is quite a bit of speculation that since the era of big money apparel contracts crash-landed into the game, the mere thought of taking the field with one less logo would be contract shoeicide. But theories aside, yes, it is still legal.

To preface the breakdown when referring to Special Teams' specialized positions, the *depth charts will read:

- *Position (K, P, LS, H, PR, KR, KO)*
- *String: First, Second, and in some cases, a Third*

The Breakdown

Let's go straight down the line, and start with the Place Kicker. This is the guy who *kicks off, kicks the PAT's (point after the touchdown), and field goals. While it sounds simple, there is a certain psychology that goes into it.

Let's take former Boise State PK, Kyle Brotzman for example. Brotzman had an insane career with the Broncos, having put up a grand total of 439 points from 2007-2010, shattering the NCAA record for most points scored by a D-1 kicker. By definition, he played *lights out* for his team, and coach Chris Petersen.

Something very unfortunate happened to put a huge stain on his record, however. On November 26, 2010 Boise State played the Nevada Wolf Pack in Reno, Nevada, who went into the game 11-1 (with their only loss of the season at Hawaii, on October

~ Positions ~

16). With a primetime ESPN TV spot, and the entire country watching, analysts said that if there was a team who could beat Boise State that season, it was Nevada.

The first 30 minutes were a slaughter, and at the half, BSU was up 21-7, but in the second half of play, Nevada came back and evened out the score, at 31-points apiece. With Mackay Stadium on fire amidst a frigid night, and :13 seconds left in regulation, BSU QB Kellen Moore hit WR Titus Young on a 54-yard pass to the Nevada nine-yard line. Considering Brotzman's record, you could cut the emotional tension with a knife as he set up to boot it in. At first and goal on the nine-yard line, Brotzman's 26-yarder sailed wide right, and missed.

To make a long story short, the game went into *overtime, and after orchestrating a drive to set Brotzman up to boot it up the middle, he missed, again; this time, from 29-yards out. Nevada *walk-on PK Anthony Martinez hit a 34-yard FG from fourth and two at the BSU 17-yard line to end it with a final score of 34-31, Nevada.

Brotzman subsequently received death threats as a result of his two botched kicks.

This example should change your opinion on how many things could go wrong for kickers. Players wait so long for their moments to do something heroic, and things like this can be devastating to their legacy. Whenever analysts speak of Boise State, aside from Kellen Moore's prolific college career, there's no avoiding the discussion of what happened that night in Reno.

One PK who always gets my attention, is Robbie Gould of the Chicago Bears. In his eight years in the league – and as of the

2012 season – Gould made 208 field goals, and hit 278 extra points, making the former Penn State Nittany Lion one of the most accurate kickers in NFL history.

Otherwise, some of the most popular kickers in football are 2011 NCAA National Champion Cade Foster from Alabama, and former New Orleans Saints' kicker John Kasay – who was the oldest, with 22 years of experience. On May 7, 2013, Kasay signed a one-day contract with the Carolina Panthers (where he played from 1995-2010) and announced his retirement.

When the ball is dropped and kicked, it's a punt, and comes off the foot of the Punter. This happens on fourth down situations that are high-risk for fear of missing the down, and having to turn the ball over with optimal field position. Or when the offense is out of field goal range.

There's a term in football called the "Coffin Corner", which are the four points on the field in the endzones where the pylons (orange markers in all four corners of the endzone) are.

The goal of the punter is to get the ball out, on, or around that point, because it sets the team up to start at their own one-yard line, and (as we discussed at the beginning of the book with the Giants/Patriots) can cause a safety. Or even better, if the ball is fumbled or intercepted, it can easily be taken in by the defense for a score.

While every team has its punting stars, a name that needs to be known by everyone is Jerrel Wilson, who spent fifteen seasons with the Kansas City Chiefs from 1963-1977. Wilson was inducted into the Chiefs Hall of Fame in 1988 for his contributions, which include (but are not limited to) four punts of over 70-yards, and a record 1,014 total punts, for the three-time Pro Bowler.

We're going to blow through the rest of these positions, because they're relatively cut and dry.

The job of the Holder, is to hold the ball after it's snapped for the kicker to boot it. Often times you'll see QB's acting as the holder due to the uncertainty of where the ball will end up. If, for whatever reason the kick is botched, the QB is at the ready to recover and find a receiver if necessary.

The job of the Long Snapper is to snap the shit out of the ball with perfectly centered accuracy to the Holder for Place Kicks. Remember that punts are drop kicks, and require no other personnel to assist in the kick.

The positions I've already listed are on the Kicking Team, who becomes the defense once the ball leaves the foot. But there's a position that is Special Team's specific for the Receiving Team: The Kick Returner, whose job is to get under the ball, field it, or return it on kickoffs and Punt Returners, who have the same job, except for punts. These positions are usually occupied by WR's, and are called *Return Specialists*.

Vocabulary

- ***Overtime***: when the game is tied after 60 minutes (NFL, CFB, CFL) of regulation (48 for high school), a coin is tossed to decide who will elect to go first, or defer (allow the other team to go first to gauge their strategy if it goes into 2OT, or more). Each team has a chance to score, which starts at the 10-yard line in high school, and the 25-yard line in college/NFL. There is no game clock, but the play clock rules are the same as regulation, and each team is given one possession. NFL OT rules are different, where there is only one OT, which runs 15 minutes. Since the NFL started regular season OT in 1974, there had only been 17 games to end in a tie – until No.18, (as previously discussed) on Sunday November 11, 2012, when the St. Louis Rams played at San Francisco.

- *Walk On*: refers to College Football, and is a player who is on the team, but not on scholarship.

- *Fake Punt*: is a punt, without the punt. Huh? Ok, so imagine all the procedures of the punt: how they line up, and under what circumstances. Well, when it's a fake punt, the punter either runs it downfield, or passes it off to a receiver. It's rare, and designed to exploit weaknesses in defenses, but it's an act of desperation.

- *Fake Field Goal*: is a trick play, and the same as a Fake Punt, except for the procedure. The ball is snapped back as it normally would, except either the PK, or Holder drops back and (hopefully) passes it to a receiver for the six, or first down, as opposed to the three. If it's a fake PAT, it then becomes a:

- *Two-Point Conversion*: in the event a TD has been made, and a team decides to "go for two", this is what it's called. The offense sets up like they would on any other down, and says a prayer that the QB hits his target. This is riskier than the PAT, but single points will win football games and prevent 2OT's if the opponent has already scored a TD, plus a PAT.

- *Onside Kick*: is when the kicking team attempts to retrieve their own ball after it's kicked off. This is kind of an act of desperation, but there are rules that apply. It has to travel at least 10-yards. Meaning, that it cannot be touched. If the ball is untouched and goes out of bounds, an automatic five-yard penalty is assessed against the kicking team.

- *Squib Kick*: is a ball that's kicked low to the ground on purpose, and typically bounces before the returner fields it. It's an effective strategy to hold off big returns, because of how unpredictable the bounce of a football is.

- *Pooch Kick*: is a kick that is intentionally hit without full power, because the return team has some badass personnel, who are notorious for returning with big yardage (or gains).

- *Free Kick*: is when a catch is fairly made by the receiving team, and they elect to attempt a FG from where the ball was spotted dead. The rules are that there is no snap, or tee, the ball must be drop kicked (punted), or the kicker may have the assistance of a holder, and the defense has to be 10-yards away from the line of scrimmage. This is rare, and while it's been attempted many times, the last successful event occurred on November 21, 1976, where Ray Wersching of the San Diego Chargers hit it from 45-yards out against the Buffalo Bills.

- *Icing The Kicker*: is such a bitch and wastes time, but happens often. This just means that when a kicking team is dialing in and waiting for the snap, the opposing head coach calls a timeout. This is intended to make the kicker nervous on his second attempt, but rarely does.

- *Fair Catch*: is when the returner motions that he will not be advancing the football. This signal renders the ball

"dead", and also protects the returner from getting hit.

Chapter Four
College Football

Despite being run like a business, College Football is the last "pure" form of the game. Players work their asses off in high school to get noticed and pursued by recruiters, and hopefully the university he grew up loving, or worshipping, is on that narrowed-down list come National Signing Day in February.

America has this never-ending love affair with college ball, because there are hundreds of colleges throughout the country, whereas, there are only 32 NFL cities and teams. The accessibility makes it easy for fans to grow up with unwavering, emotional attachments to their local products and colleges.

If you attended college, or are enrolled currently, you know the mood this game puts you in. From rivalry weeks, Homecoming Week and more, seeing the fraternities, sororities, and campus decorated, the bonfires, and rallies with the team before big games. The ability to interact with players, attend classes with them, walk from your dorms to the stadium, and be part of something so amazing is what truly captures our hearts and minds. However silly this "culture" might seem to outsiders, we don't really care because it's our school, it's what we love, and why we wear our colors so proudly.

While most of us know college football from the aesthetic veneer of beer, cannons, beer, fight songs, more beer, cheerleaders, beer, tailgating, whiskey, and quarterbacks, it's really a complicated nervous system that's just waiting to combust.

This chapter will explain everything from high school recruiting, eligibility, the scandals that have rocked college athletics, to Championships and Bowl Games.

High School Recruiting

The NCAA has 120 Division-1 Member Institutions (schools) that are split up by subdivisions:

- *FBS (Football Bowl Subdivision): where teams can have 85 scholarship athletes on their rosters, with 25 new scholarships awarded every year.*

- *FCS (Football Championship Subdivision): are allowed 63 full scholarships, a few partials, and 30 new scholarships per year, as long as they don't exceed 85 total roster spots.*

According to the National Collegiate Athletics Association (NCAA), only 5.8 percent, or 1 out of every 17 high school players will advance to the collegiate level (all sports), and only 1, in 16,000 high school athletes will have a professional career in sports. If obtaining a scholarship isn't an option, people should use that metric to gauge their planning, in terms of additional training to get a competitive edge.

Scholarships are offered the same way athletes get noticed: through available game film (to see how valuable they could be to the team), and what the coaches and recruiters like, based off of observation periods.

While skill is important in assessing talent, recruiters and coaches also factor in character, academic, and criminal backgrounds – to name a few – which can, and will work against the player, if the college considers him a risk.

Verbal Commitments are a vague topic, and in my opinion, the whole process is a lot of hype. It's when an athlete verbally commits to a college or university – usually during his junior year, or the summer going into his senior season. The player has no contractually binding agreement at this point, and can change his mind as many times as he wishes, up until the time he signs his *Letter of Intent.

Observation Periods (or Evaluation Periods) mean that the recruiter can only assess the player based on his academics, and athletics, with zero contact.

For the bulk of the high school players' season, he has no interaction with recruiters, but from November to January is *Contact Period, and from the end of January up until the day after *National Signing Day on February 1, there are off-and-on *Quiet Periods, and *Dead Periods. It should be noted that Letters of Intent for football, continue up until April 1.

To make a really long (four-year process) short, on National Signing Day, the athlete signs, and sends in a legally binding contract with the NCAA, and the respective member institution he signed with, called a Letter of Intent.

There's a provisionary option called Early Enrollment, which means the athlete has met the high school graduation requirements early, and can enroll in the university he has signed with, typically in the spring semester – or third quarter

– depending on how the institution's academic calendar is configured.

There are a few things to know about the LOI, however. The contract is an agreement that says, if the student-athlete leaves that school, he'll likely lose financial aid, and could be sidelined for an entire season if he transfers elsewhere. There is a grace period of a few days after signing the LOI for a student-athlete to back out, and void the contract. This is often the case for student-athletes who are pressured, but if that's not the case, be prepared for a backlash, because reasonings are pretty transparent for recruiters and coaches, and they're not stupid. Athletes can request to be released from their LOI, but this is rare, and it's even less likely that should this occur, the school comply with the request.

Just because a student-athlete has signed an LOI, doesn't guarantee the scholarship, especially if his grades slip in the final semester of high school, and he doesn't meet the NCAA's academic eligibility requirements. Please remember how imperative it is, that school remain a central focus for the duration of his amateur career, as scholarships are also renewed yearly.

Obviously this is just the core of what goes into the process, but the best place to seek counsel and advice on the topic are through high school coaches. Seeking outside guidance or anything to that extent could be deemed a recruiting violation, which will be discussed a few sections down.

Over the years, I've observed how little people care about National Signing Day, which is sad. If fans watched high school all-star games, they'd be able to see the future of their college teams unfolding right on those very fields. When fans head to their school's pages on ESPN and click on the Recruiting icons, those one, two, three, four, and five-star commits would have them salivating if they understood how big of an asset, or impact player they could be, and what their talent could develop into. I've seen it time, and time again, where an athlete will have an outstanding play in a game, and fans ask, "where did this kid come from?" When these athletes fax in their Letters of Intent (LOI) to their respective universities every February, fans should make it a point to know several key facts about them. If you do your homework, watching them take off in college will be so much more rewarding.

Vocabulary

- **Contact Period**: a time period when recruiters can have contact with the recruit, and his parents.

- **Quiet Period**: a 42-day period from September, through November when recruits can visit campuses, and coaches can have in-person, off campus visits with recruits.

- **Dead Period**: when there is absolutely zero contact whatsoever, under any circumstance, between recruits and coaches.

- **Letter of Intent**: (NLI), is a legally binding contract between the player and the institution through the NCAA, that declares where he will be attending, and playing college football. An NLI can also be voided if the player requests to delay enrollment, or is asked to delay his entry (for whatever reason), then the athlete is released, and can sign elsewhere without penalty.

I'm a big fan of books, so if you, or any family members have any additional questions, concerns, or want the "inside" angle of the world of recruiting, check out *Meat Market,* by CBS Sports analyst and writer, Bruce Feldman.

I recommend following recruiting analysts on Twitter, and ESPN has an excellent team of conference-specific analysts on Recruiting Nation, who offer "mail bags", or open forums to discuss issues, athletes, and more.

The NCAA: National Collegiate Athletics Association

Let's jump right in, with the explanation of how the NCAA was founded, who they are, and what they do.

The NCAA was founded when Teddy Roosevelt called upon the leaders of college athletics to the White House, to discuss ways to reform the early "Bloody Monday" forms of Football, and create a governing committee to enforce the new set of rules and guidelines.

In December 1906, following a meeting that was moderated by Chancellor Henry MacCracken of New York University (which hasn't had a football team since 1952), a congregation of 62 universities declared the inaugural institution of the Intercollegiate Athletic Association of the United States. The name was changed in 1910, to the NCAA.

That's the basic explanation, but if you ever wish further your expertise regarding the NCAA and its history, I recommend reading *The Big Scrum,* by John J. Miller.

At this point, the NCAA is made up of all of its member institutions, that are the universities and colleges they govern. If anything ever seems unfair, just remember, there are roughly 335 institutions (including FBS, FCS, and D-1 programs that don't have football programs) who fuel this machine.

If your school has ever been impacted by the NCAA, or you know of an athlete who has had issues with them, initial thoughts are that they ought to be renamed the "N-C-Double Assholes", but they do have some good intentions. Although, ask any football, baseball, softball, or basketball player his, or her take on them, versus a tennis player, or other sport that isn't considered a big money-maker to a school, and the differences in opinions might shock you.

So, what exactly do they do? They enforce, regulate, determine eligibility, sanction, and dump about 90 percent of the funding back into its member institutions.

Just a side note, other organizations do exist, and include the National Junior College Athletic Association, the NAIA, and the National Christian College Athletics Association, just to name a few.

NCAA Clearinghouse

This is a separate governing and enforcement committee within the NCAA, who focus solely on academic eligibility. If a player doesn't get the grades in high school, they won't be cleared by the NCAA. This is why so many highly rated, *blue chip athletes end up taking the Junior College (JuCo) routes, where they have to obtain their associates degrees in order to transfer to a university.

The Clearinghouse also determines if international athletes are cleared to play in the United States, as well as clearing student-athletes to participate in events, such as the Olympics.

Vocabulary

- *Blue Chip*: a top prospect student-athlete.

Scandals and Sanctions

Scandals are touchy subjects, and most big schools have felt the pains they bring, by the sanctions they get slapped with, for whatever infraction, or violation they committed at some point.

Four years ago, I conducted surveys throughout the country on former student-athletes regarding the NCAA, and an alarmingly high number of participants said they were never explained the rules, or fine print that went along with their contracts. Moreover, many of the participants noted they were from families who were living at, or under the poverty level, and were receiving government assistance via food stamps. Likewise, many of these participants strongly felt their careers were jeopardized through coaching changes or problems that stemmed from the NCAA's lack of full transparency.

In regards to coaching changes, they can leave any program, at any time, for whatever reason, and without penalty. The only exception to this, is with a "show cause" levied through NCAA sanctions following investigations, that typically bans a coach from NCAA institutions for several years.

The most common infractions committed are:

- **Failure to Monitor**: is when an institution fails to adequately monitor rules.

- **Lack of Institutional Control**: is when an institution extensively fails to monitor rules, or outright ignores them.

- **Improper Benefits**: includes anything that separates amateurism, from professionalism. The NCAA rules have always been vague on this, and others, but always seem to get scrutinized every time they hand this down because they claim they don't play "favoritism", but fans, and institutions beg to differ. IB's are anything from being paid to play (monetary compensation), receiving gifts from employees or boosters, and the list goes on. In trying to enforce this, critics say the NCAA has gone too far in trying to maintain amateurism, when student-athletes are living off of stipends, that in some cases, don't even cover half their monthly overhead, with rent and bills, even if they're on full-ride scholarships. It really is a sick, almost inhumane practice, and this opinion is based on extensive field research.

Regarding Improper Benefits, the argument many have, is that student-athletes *are* paid, via "free" tuition, room, board, and training tables (one "free" meal per day). But what athletes are doing to their bodies, and the risks they take daily, are hardly considered a fair trade off. To anyone who doesn't quite understand what I'm talking about, first, go contract a linebacker to clothesline you after running 30-yards at full speed, while slamming you into the turf. Then, while you're in severe pain, realize that athletes' are expected to perform on a filet mignon level, while they're on a $.99 menu budget, and if they even accept a slice of pizza without paying for it, or a recruit is given more than one cream cheese spread with their bagel on a visit, they run the risk of committing a violation. That sounds fair, doesn't it?

If you were to look up any of the violations listed, you'd find quite a few institutions, because of how vague the NCAA is at explaining things, and how little players are actually taught. Now, don't get me wrong, some of the things schools get slapped with regarding IB's are for legitimate reasons, but the argument of "Why didn't *they* get charged with, what *we* got charged with, for committed practically the same thing?" arises all too often, and until the NCAA lightens up, or stops using language that student-athletes, or their parents need attorneys to translate, nothing will change.

One thing the NCAA does make sure to put into English, are the picture diagrams throughout their website. The best one I found, explained the process of charging in major infractions cases; which says the NCAA notifies the institution of the "allegations", based on the conclusion of their investigations. If the institution accepts, they either self-impose sanctions that require approval, or the NCAA makes it rain. The institution can also request a hearing, in which both sides go back and forth with evidence and questioning, much like a courtroom. Then the committee releases a report with their findings, and penalties are hammered down. The institution is given the option to accept, in which the case is closed, or they appeal, and step two is repeated. Did I mention the NCAA is usually the plaintiff, the jury, AND the judge?

Here are a few universities who have been hit the hardest by sanctions:

Southern Methodist University in Dallas, Texas was investigated initially in the early 70s, up until the time they were handed down the Death Penalty. This was because they continually posted winning records, and managed to land all of the nation's top recruits, which raised red flags. Subsequently, the Mustangs were put on probation for recruiting violations in 1985 for (but not limited to) several large cash bribes, which the school, and administrators knew about – including Texas Governor Bill Clements.

While SMU was already under sanctions, another scandal was revealed, that there was a slush fund provided by university boosters, which paid out 13 players around $60,000 in one year. Considering the exorbitant nature of the violations, the NCAA had no choice but to hand down the worse type of sentence a school could be dealt: The Death Penalty.

To make another long story short, the penalties included the cancellation of the 1987 season, along with cancellations of all home games the following season (which the school had no choice but to cancel), they were stripped of 55 scholarships over four years, their coaching staff was reduced to four, their existing probation was extended until the 1990 season, and their recruiting methods were screwed until 1989.

Existing players were allowed to transfer without penalty, making the campus a circus, and as a result of the shitstorm of sanctions, SMU didn't get back to being competitive until the 2009 season, where they met Nevada at the Sheraton Hawaii Bowl and won, 45-10.

The University of Southern California scandal, involving star running back (and former Kim Kardashian mancandy) Reggie Bush, pales in comparison to SMU, but it's still a scandal that is highly discussed because of the program it happened to, and what they lost as a result.

The NCAA found that Reggie Bush was in violation of his amateur status because he, and his family, had accepted gifts upwards of $100,000, including a San Diego home, from sports marketers and agent Lloyd Lake, and Michael Michaels, during Bush's time at SC.

The reason this was investigated in the first place was because Lake and Michaels went to media with the allegations because the Bush camp wouldn't pay back the money given to them, when Bush signed with a different agency upon declaring for the NFL Draft, when Bush had allegedly promised to sign with them. As a result of the NCAA ruling in favor of the allegations, USC was handed down the harshest penalty to a D-1 university (until Penn State in 2012), that included a post-season bowl ban from 2010-2011, the loss of 30 scholarships over three years, the loss of their 2004 National Championship – which remains vacated in the record books – and all wins during the 2005 season.

Reggie Bush also returned his Heisman trophy – the only player in history to return the nation's most coveted college trophy.

The Ohio State University scandal was pretty extensive, but here is a condensed version to highlight the major reasons they were being investigated. The university launched an internal investigation into football players, Terrelle Pryor, Dan Herron, DeVeir Posey, Solomon Thomas, and Mike Adams for their involvement in selling memorabilia, and exchanging awards for tattoos, and other improper benefits.

Upon conclusion in December of 2010, the players were suspended for the first five games of the 2011 season. After the season ended, media reported that the Buckeyes' highly decorated, sweater-vest wearing head coach Jim Tressel, knew his players were violating NCAA rules on IB's months before the school was tipped off, and said nothing about it. Because of this, Tressel was fined $250,000, and suspended for the first two games of the 2011 season.

Where it gets complicated, is that there were emails forwarded to Ted Sarniak (Pryor's "mentor"), by Tressel, after it was brought to his attention that players were in a possible drug probe. That's when Tressel failed to report the allegations to school, and NCAA officials. Then the NCAA got tipped off, that Ohio State players – including Pryor – were violating IB's in the form of the usage of vehicles from a local car dealership, where a former player admitted to local Columbus media, that he had exchanged memorabilia for a car. Due to the amount of evidence that piled up against Tressel, he resigned in May 2011, and within months, Ohio State's sanctions were handed down: The NCAA accepted the Buckeyes' self-imposed sanctions which were a two-year post season ban, but added the vacation of wins from the 2010 season, along with their win against Arkansas in the Sugar Bowl that season.

Ironically, the Buckeyes went undefeated in 2012 under head coach Urban Meyer.

The University of Miami investigation initially began in 1994, when the NCAA found that several NFL players, and rapper, 2 Live Crew's Luther Campbell, were paying Miami players for things ranging from big hits, to scoring. The NCAA also declared the staff knew, and in that same year, Tony Russell (Miami's Academic Advisor at the time), plead guilty to tampering and lying on applications for Pell Grants, and 23 scholarships for 57 players, which defrauded the Pell Grant Program of more than $220,000. There were a few more incidents through the 90s against The U, but the most recent began around 2010, and is still active, involving former Hurricane's booster, Nevin Shapiro, who is currently serving a 20-year sentence in prison for securities fraud and money laundering (Ponzi scheme), in which he swindled investors for around $930 million. Shapiro defrauded more than 50 investors, ranging from $50 million to over $100 million, when he was "selling" his company as a wholesale grocery distribution company.

On August 20, 2010, Shapiro donated over $143 million to the University of Miami (who returned over $130 million to the court appointed bankruptcy trust), after pleading guilty to the Ponzi scheme. But as a key player to the development of the program, a lot of the blame and speculation went against the University itself, because nobody seemed to take responsibility for their actions in knowing what was going on. The investigation went on for a year, but there is a four-year statue of limitations, so most of the allegations involving the U's athletes, and Shapiro are exempt from violations.

Yahoo! broke this story initially, by Sports Chief Investigator, Charles Robinson, who also broke the Ohio State news. Robinson spent 1,000 hours conducting interviews with Shapiro, and reviewed over 20,000 pages of business records, as well as 5,000 pages of cell phone records and over 1,000 photos.

Everything from cash, prostitutes, jewelry, trips, yacht outings, cash for injuries (bounties), and even an abortion for a Miami players' girlfriend, were part of evidence against Shapiro.

Allegedly, seven Miami coaches and assistants knew, but turned a blind eye instead of reporting them to Compliance, or the Athletic Director.

From 2002-2010, Shapiro claimed to have given around $2 million in illegal benefits to 72 University of Miami athletes, and coaches, committing quite possibly the longest laundry list of NCAA violations known to date; from extra benefits, to impermissible compensation to coaches.

Shapiro is allegedly writing a book in prison, which is said to be a detailed dossier on Miami, and how they were able to get away with their actions for so long. Shapiro also claims, "Once the players turned pro, they turned their back on me. It made me feel like a used friend".

Upon conclusion of the NCAA's formal investigation on August 25, 2011, they declared 13 players ineligible. Miami petitioned this, but only one player, Marcus Robinson, was cleared. The NCAA said that players would be required to make restitution before they would be reinstated, and be eligible to play. This ranged from $100 - $1,200. The players who had received the least in payments were not suspended, but two players were suspended for four games, with one serving a six game suspension.

Paul Dee had served on the Committee of Infractions for USC's investigation (see above), and was also Miami's Athletic Director at the time, so you can only imagine how infuriated Trojan faithful were at the hypocrisy upon this news being released.

There are several inconsistencies within the investigation (through a media perspective), and several "Dee-like" instances, but allegedly, former Miami head coach Randy Shannon (fired in 2010) wanted nothing to do with Shapiro, and warned his staff and players of him.

Pending the NCAA's Notice of Allegations, and conclusion of their initial investigation on November 20, 2011, Miami announced that they were self-imposing bowl (game) consideration for the 2011 and 2012 seasons, and elected to withdraw from consideration in playing in the ACC Championship Game.

On February 19, 2013, the NCAA sent Miami its Notice of Allegations, where UM President Donna Shalala issued a response, stating that The U "deeply regrets and takes full responsibility for those NCAA violations that are based on fact and are corroborated by multiple individuals and/or documentation." Shalala went on in her statement to reiterate self-imposed bans and restrictions, as well as detailing the investigation – which is still ongoing as of September 2013.

Penn State University: The most recent scandal is one that nobody saw coming, and definitely one that hits everyone who grew up following the Nittany Lions, and celebrating never-ending years of Joe Paterno wins. Joe Pa's legacy was built on strong fundamentals of honor, integrity, courage, and more, and for years he preached the importance of values, and ethics.

In 1969, Jerry Sandusky joined Paterno's staff coaching the defensive line. About a decade later, Sandusky formed a non-profit called Second Mile, which was (on the surface) a foundation to help underprivileged and neglected children. From 1994-2006, Sandusky met, preyed, and sexually molested/raped a number of young boys all in the age range from 7- 13 years old. The biggest problems that were uncovered throughout this investigation, were the amount of people who knew, and witnessed these acts happening, but did nothing to stop them.

Everyone from the custodial staff (Jim Calhoun), to Mike McQueary – who was a former player, and graduate assistant knew. According to reports, McQueary reported what he saw in the Penn State Locker Room to Paterno, who reported it to Tim Curley (the Athletic Director), and Graham Spanier (the University President), who decide not to report the incident to authorities. In 2008, one of Sandusky's victims came forward, which resulted in an extensive investigation by the Grand Jury.

Paterno, McQueary, Curley and Spanier were subpoenaed to testify that no report was ever made of the incident. The tireless investigation culminated on November 5, 2011 when Jerry Sandusky was arrested on charges of sexually abusing eight boys, and posted a $100,000 bail after his arraignment.

Two days later, Graham Spanier and Tim Curley resigned after being charged with perjury and failure to report. On November 9, Paterno announced that he would be resigning at the end of the season, but the board fired him shortly after his announcement. A month later, Paterno announced that he had lung cancer, and passed away on January 22, 2012.

During the eleven days of the trial (in June 2012), Matt Sandusky – Jerry's own adopted son – announced that he, too, had been a victim, and the next day, Sandusky was convicted on 45 of the 48 counts of sexual abuse, where the 68-year old was eligible for a maximum sentence of 442 years in prison.

In the months following the trial, former FBI director and judge, Louis Freeh released a report based off an independent investigation, which prompted a swift reaction by the NCAA to impose sanctions to Penn State. In light of this, the university took action, and removed the 600-pound bronze statue of Joe Paterno, (designed by Angel Di Maria) that stood outside Beaver Stadium, which was the iconic focal point of the campus.

On July 23, 2012, the nation stood silent as the NCAA listed off their sanctions (that analysts deemed to be worse than the Death Penalty): the vacation of ALL wins from 1998-2011, $60 million in fines, with reduced scholarships (down to 65), and a post-season bowl ban for the next four years. This also opened the floodgates for players to be able to transfer without penalty, meaning they were eligible for immediate play.

On October 9, 2012, Sandusky was sentenced 30-60 years in prison, and ordered to pay trial costs. Several of the victims have launched formal lawsuits against the university since.

Fans and critics argued extensively that sanctions were meant to punish Penn State by crippling it financially, which was unfair to the players, as they had personally done nothing wrong. This furthers the argument that college football is a business, and if sanctioning a team by stripping scholarships doesn't shed light on the fact that education is secondary in this empire, nothing will. If the NCAA upheld all scholarships, yet limited players who could dress, that would be fair. But reducing scholarships prevents many athletes from receiving an education, which seems a bit counterproductive, all things considered.

As a side note, any situation involving children being sexually exploited needs to be addressed to the FBI and local law enforcement immediately. No exceptions. Protect those who can't protect themselves.

Who Dominates Division-1

While every fan has their opinion on "who's the best", statistics, winning percentages, award winners, bowl winners, National Championships, and all the surrounding components certainly do not lie when deciphering this.

When describing prolific teams in the sports world, the term "dynasty" will reign supreme in the intro, and in any context. While most of us refer to USC, Alabama, Texas, Florida, Ohio State and other programs as dynasties, they still fall well short of the record 19 championships that Yale put up from 1874-1909. While football is risky to this day, remember, those guys played with zero rules, and canvas and leather uniforms.

Most will argue the SEC is the most dominant, and to some extent that's true, but let's take a look at who's dominated what, over the past few years.

Individual statistics such as passing yards, rushing yards, receiving yards, tackles, sacks, interceptions, field goals made versus attempted, PAT's, and others, are very much individual stats; but football isn't. If a team has a badass QB, but his receivers can't catch for shit, he has no stats. Likewise, if the WR has shit hands, the QB's stats are going to suck for that game. I've seen it happen, which is why accuracy is the most stressed factor with QB's.

In terms of winning percentages, only a fraction of D-1 teams have registered a consistent winning season percentage of over .600, but the big name schools who have achieved this with at least 100 games, are Michigan, Alabama, Ohio State, Florida A&M, Nebraska, USC, Boise State, Texas, and Notre Dame.

Due to Penn State's sanctions following the Sandusky investigation, the school was stripped of 111 wins, giving Paterno 298, of his 409. As a result, former Florida State Seminoles head coach (1976-2009) Bobby Bowden, was put in the top spot as the winningest coach in history, with 377 NCAA-recognized wins. Bowden isn't credited for 22 wins at South Georgia Junior College (1956-1958), plus five wins from 2006, and seven wins from 2007, which were vacated as a result of NCAA finding that there were academic violations on his squads for those years.

There are several awards given to the nation's top football players every year. These awards are extensive, so here's a list of the big ones, with their winners from the 2009-2012 seasons.

1. *The Dick Butkus Award (Outstanding Linebacker, also given annually to a professional, and high school athlete):*

    2012: Manti Te'o – Notre Dame (Independent)

    2011: Luke Kuechly – Boston College (ACC)

    2010: Von Miller – Texas A&M (Big 12)

    2009: Rolando McClain – Alabama (SEC)

~ College Football ~

2. *The Jim Thorpe Award (most outstanding DB):*

   2012: Johnthan Banks – Mississippi State (SEC)

   2011: Morris Claiborne – Louisiana State University (SEC)

   2010: Patrick Peterson – Louisiana State University (SEC)

   2009: Eric Berry – Tennessee (SEC)

3. *The Outland Trophy (Outstanding Interior Linemen):*

   2012: Luke Joeckel – Texas A&M (SEC)

   2011: Barrett Jones – Alabama (SEC)

   2010: Gabe Carimi – Wisconsin (Big 10)

   2009: Ndamukong Suh – Nebraska (Big 10)

4. *The Walter Camp Award (Player of the Year):*

   2012: LB Manti Te'o – Notre Dame (Independent)

   2011: QB Andrew Luck – Stanford (Pac 12)

   2010: QB Cam Newton – Auburn (SEC)

   2009: QB Colt McCoy – Texas (Big 12)

5. *The Fred Biletnikoff Award (Outstanding Wide Receiver:*

   2012: Marqise Lee – USC (Pac 12)

   2011: Justin Blackmon – Oklahoma State (Big 12)

   2010: Justin Blackmon – Oklahoma State (Big 12)

   2009: Golden Tate – Notre Dame (Independent)

6. *The Johnny Unitas Golden Arm Award (Outstanding Senior Quarterback):*

    2012: Collin Klein – Kansas State (Big 12) – Who didn't even get drafted in the 2013 NFL Draft.

    2011: Andrew Luck – Stanford (Pac 12)

    2010: Scott Tolzien – Wisconsin (Big 10)

    2009: Colt McCoy – Texas (Big 12)

7. *The Maxwell Award (Outstanding Player):*

    2012: LB Manti Te'o – Notre Dame (Independent)

    2011: QB Andrew Luck – Stanford (Pac 12)

    2010: QB Cam Newton – Auburn (SEC)

    2009: QB Colt McCoy – Texas (Big 12)

8. *The Doak Walker Award (National Running Back Award):*

    2012: Montee Ball – Wisconsin (Big 10)

    2011: Trent Richardson – Alabama (SEC)

    2010: LaMichael James – Oregon (Pac 12)

    2009: Toby Gerhart – Stanford (Pac 12)

The Heisman is the most highly sought after, and coveted award a player could achieve in his amateur career. This award was founded in 1935, and for 76 years, has been the celebratory focal point for the nation's most outstanding college football player. Every December, finalists congregate in New York City for the presentation from the Heisman Trust.

~ College Football ~

Heisman Winners from the past decade are:

1. 2003: QB Jason White, Oklahoma
2. 2004: QB Matt Leinart, USC
3. 2005: RB Reggie Bush, USC (vacated)
4. 2006: QB Troy Smith, Ohio State
5. 2007: QB Tim Tebow, Florida
6. 2008: QB Sam Bradford, Oklahoma
7. 2009: RB Mark Ingram, Alabama
8. 2010: QB Cam Newton, Auburn
9. 2011: QB Robert Griffin III, Baylor
10. 2012: QB Johnny "Football" Manziel, Texas A&M (first freshmen to win the Heisman Trophy.)

As you can see based off these awards alone, the powerhouse conferences in college football are the SEC, Pac 12, Big 12, and the Big 10.

Polls

There are several polls that decide where the top 25 of the nation's best teams rank, based off the strength of schedules, and wins/losses, but they're all determined by different professionals in the industry to level the idea of favoritism out. The three polls are the AP (Associated Press), the Coaches' Poll (determined by college football coaches), and the BCS Standings, which are determined by a complex computer/human polling system.

~ College Football ~

Bowls

You should have noticed by now, that there are a lot of vacated wins by teams who have competed in Bowl Games, so they're obviously a big deal. But why? Money.

Here's a list of a few, to give you an idea of how big the payouts are:

- The Outback Bowl is usually played on New Year's Day, between teams from the SEC, and Big 10 conferences in Tampa Bay, Florida at Raymond James Stadium (Home of the NFC - South, Tampa Bay Buccaneers): $7,400,000.

- The Buffalo Wild Wings Bowl played at Sun Devil Stadium (home to the Arizona State Sun Devils) featuring the third place teams from the Big 12, and Big 10 conferences, after BCS selections have been made: $3,300,000.

- The Chick-Fil-A Bowl, featuring teams from the ACC and the SEC, and the ninth-oldest bowl game, which is played in Atlanta, Georgia (At the Georgia Dome, which is home to the NFC - South Atlanta Falcons): $3,350,000.

So how are post-season games determined? It's a two-part system, but to put it as simply as possible, there are 40 bowl games available to play in, and FBS teams within specific conferences are automatic qualifiers. These teams have to post a certain number of wins, among other variables to be eligible, and then the teams are narrowed down. How I figure it, is that if there are 120 FBS members and 40 bowl games, 80 of them will be participating in bowls. The second part is the different bowl games who have contracts with conferences that determine who will play in them. For example, the Rose Bowl in Pasadena,

California has contracts (called "tie-ins") with the Pac 12, and the Big 10 conferences. The top teams from the Pac 12 and Big 10 are first to be invited, but if a team is obligated to the BCS National Championship game, either an at-large team fills the spot, or a second place, in-conference team is invited.

Just so you're clear on who the automatic qualifying (AQ) conferences are: The ACC, Big 12, Big Ten, SEC, and Pac 12.

BCS: Bowl Championship Series

A separate series of five bowls, that includes the nation's top ten teams (aside from the BCS National Championship teams) are called the BCS Bowl Championship Series. As stated previously, these teams are selected by a computer/human polling system, and are based off the same factors as the season ranking polls, but also the champions from the AQ conferences listed above, plus, FBS Independent schools who qualify.

The BCS National Championship

This game is main stage, prime time, and big money ($18,000,000 payout), that involves the nation's top two teams, who's participation is based on the final Coaches' Poll of the season, plus computer rankings, and the Harris Poll, which is a collaboration of former players, coaches, and current media elitists. Although, it's pretty easy to gauge what teams will be in attendance, if you're following the season.

Some of the top winning teams, and their respective conferences include LSU (SEC), Oklahoma, Texas (Big 12), USC (Pac 12), and the Big 10 (Ohio State). But it's mainly dominated by the SEC with eight wins from Tennessee, Florida, LSU, and Auburn, with Alabama being the most recent winner, with back-to-back wins in 2012, when the Crimson Tide went hunting, and beat the LSU Tigers, 21-0, and at Sun Life Stadium in Miami, Florida on January 7, 2013, when quarterback A.J. McCarron and the Tide routed Notre Dame, 42-14.

The Vizio 2014 BCS National Championship will be held at The Rose Bowl in Pasadena, California on Monday, January 6, 2014.

In the spring of 2012, the BCS announced that starting in the 2014 season, there would be a playoff system, and on April 24, 2013, The "College Football Playoffs" name was confirmed. Following the 2013 season, the playoffs will be replacing the Bowl Championship Series to determine a National Champion.

Within a matter of minutes, I wrote this piece, which is my opinion and should be taken as a strong opinion of the author, and not intended to create mass hysteria. Or, awkward first date material:

"Most of us want to be thrilled at the new BCS Playoff System starting in 2014, but selecting the four teams is going to be a huge responsibility for the BCS Committee, who has continually managed to demonstrate chronic injudiciousness in all aspects.

Here's how it will to go down: There will be four seeded teams with semi-final games on New Years Eve/Day, followed by the National Championship (rotated between bowls) a week later, on what the Committee wants to call "Championship Monday".

How will the teams be selected? For the next 12 years (length of new contract), a Selection Committee will take the place of the highly scrutinized computer/human poll. The selections will be weighted on W-to-L, strength of schedule, and whether the teams in discussion were their respective conference champions.

The problem I have with this, is the seeding will likely be dominated by the SEC, Pac-12, B10 and Big12, so in that aspect, nothing will change.

Once again, smaller schools will be booted from qualifying because of the strength of their schedule. This is because only one school from a non-AQ in the MWC, C-USA, MAC, SBC and WAC Conferences are given an automatic berth, and this is only if the team is ranked in the Top 12, or Top 16, and higher than at least one BCS Conference Champion.

This really solves nothing for the most discerning sports enthusiasts, yet pacifies the seeding lust for couch commandos who yearn for a longer season at the expense of our sanity. It should also be noted, the site of the National Championship will be awarded to the highest bidder. So cheers to 12 years of comical drama, NCAA politics and shaft diving."

All Americans

When you read statistics on your favorite collegiate players, you'll see bullets that read "All America", or "All SEC".

The title of "All America Team" is simply referred to the top athletes in their respective positions, who are voted on by a number of reputable media agencies, such as Scout.com, Sports Illustrated, ESPN, and others.

These athletes get put on an imaginary team, because there is no All-American game.

When you see a player referenced to "All" and his conference, it's the same honor, except at a smaller scale, voted on by peers and media within the conference. Every 10 years, the conferences vote on who the best-of-the-best were, in their respective positions were for the past decade, which translates into another honor, of "All (insert conference) All-Decade" team.

Chapter Five
The National Football League

The NFL is what it all comes down to. Twenty-something years of practice, perfection, and calculated moves are culminated by whether the player has a roster spot or not, in a league that only employs 1,952 athletes. To break that number down, each of the 32 teams has a 53-man roster: 47 who dress out on game days, and 14 who are on their respective sideline in their team apparel, including the eight members on the practice squad.

If you thought the depiction of how the league calendar from several chapters back was insanity at its finest, think again.

The following chapter will be a crash course from everything business-related, to the scandals and planning that dictates roster cuts and additions, in an environment where the only thing more terrifying than an ACL tear, is the uncertainty of whether the player will have an income the next day, as a result.

The reason we obsess over this multi-billion dollar a year industry ($35 Billion in 2012, according to Forbes), is because it's made up of athletes who have proven they are the elitists, and while our emotions tend to take flight in regards to our favorite players, friends, or family members getting cut, or injured, it's part of a game that's over 100 years old, and one of the few things that truly maintains its consistency.

This emotional attachment is why most men refuse to give it

up. For many, their glory days ended after their last game as a senior in high school, but they continue to hold on, by donning their favorite players' jerseys, and insisting on playing flag football until their joints just can't handle the routs anymore. This tendency is similar to the female obsession with high-end fashion. While turning the pages of Vogue, daydreaming about Chanel ready-to-wear and Hermes Birkin Bags, we get lost in a fantasy land that's no different than the connection men make while playing Armchair Quarterback on Game Day.

History of the NFL

The National Football League debuted as the American Professional Football Association in 1920, with eleven teams. This came to be in a similar way the NCAA was born, except in Canton, Ohio. This is why the Hall of Fame is located in Canton, as a way to commemorate the city where the league's foundation was developed on.

In 1922, the NPFA became the NFL, and introduced a "winner takes all" championship title, given to the team who posted the best regular season record. The first championship games started in 1933, and by the late 50s, the NFL had surpassed Major League Baseball in television ratings.

This was a result of the 1958 championship game televised by NBC, between the Baltimore Colts and the New York Giants, held at Yankee Stadium on December 28, 1958, in front of a little more than 64,000 fans. The Colts beat the Giants 23-17, in the first game to go into sudden death overtime, and quickly received the title as "The Greatest Game Ever Played."

Before discussing the merger, the AFL (American Football League) was the secondary professional football organization in the United States, and started in 1959 with eight teams, and ended their final season in 1970, with 10.

AFL-NFL Merger 101

One of the greatest issues investors had with the NFL, was that they were in no hurry to expand or add franchises. A key player to their rival league was oil heir Lamar Hunt, who established an eight city American Football League, and tirelessly head hunted the top prospects, talent, and NFL rejects from all across the country to be as competitive as possible, despite being constantly criticized by the NFL.

Several policies that are used in modern day play that were invented by the AFL, are players' names on their jerseys, two-point conversions, official time, and television deals with ABC and NBC – two networks who remain strongly invested in football to this day.

One of the key players to initiating the merger, was Al Davis. At the time, Davis was not only the Raiders' owner, he was the AFL's Co-Commissioner, and had been very vocal in his commitment to bludgeoning the available talent pool, by instituting a vicious bidding war between the NFL for talent. At the time, NFL personnel were getting anxious at what Davis could do, so they proposed the merger to all the AFL teams without Davis' knowledge. Davis wasn't really left with an option to approve, but as a result, there were several new rules and protocols added. The primary addition was the end of the bidding war, and the institutionalization of the common draft.

In 1970, all of the AFL teams, plus three teams from the NFL, became members of the AFC (American Football Conference), with the rest of the 13 NFL teams forming the NFC (National Football Conference), and thus the modern system was born.

If you've ever taken a look at the NFL logo, you will see four stars on either side of a football, which signify the two different conferences (AFC and NFC), and their four divisions: North, South, East, and West.

The following two sections – The AFC, and The NFC – include general breakdowns, with basic information on all 32 NFL teams, by conference, and division.

The AFC

All 16 AFC teams by division, with brief background notes:

AFC – East: Buffalo Bills, Miami Dolphins, New England Patriots, and the New York Jets.

AFC – North: Baltimore Ravens, Cincinnati Bengals, Cleveland Browns, and the Pittsburgh Steelers.

AFC – South: Houston Texans, Indianapolis Colts, Jacksonville Jaguars, and the Tennessee Titans.

AFC – West: Denver Broncos, Kansas City Chiefs, Oakland Raiders, and the San Diego Chargers.

AFC – East:

The Buffalo Bills were named after William Frederick "Buffalo Bill" Cody (February 26, 1846 - January 10, 1917), who was an American soldier, Medal of Honor recipient, and hunter. The Bills are owned by Ralph Wilson, managed by Buddy Nix, and coached by Chan Galley. They are the only New York team to operate within New York State lines, where they play in Ralph Wilson Stadium, Orchard Park NY (1973 – present), with a one-game-a-year contract through 2017, in Toronto at Rogers Centre. The Bills currently hold a Playoff record of 10 wins, and 16 losses. CJ Spiller, Kyle Williams, and Jarius Byrd represented the franchise in the 2013 Pro Bowl. Another player who has had a big impact in recent years, is WR Stevie Johnson, who was Drafted in 2008 by the Bills. From 2008-2012, Johnson put up 249 receptions for 3,235 yards, and 25 receiving touchdowns. Aside from the numbers, he's known for his "Why So Serious" campaign against former Bengals' players, Terrell Owens, and Chad Ochocinco (who used to refer to themselves as "Batman and Robin"), which launched after he scored a touchdown on November 21, 2010 at Paul Brown Stadium in Cincinnati. Johnson was subsequently fined $5,000 for his undershirt-bearing stunt.

The Miami Dolphins were established in 1966 as an AFL expansion team. The Phins, or Fins, operate out of Davie, Florida, but play their games at Sun Life Stadium in Miami Gardens. They are quite possibly the most celebrity-centered team in the league, with a star power roster of marginal ownership percentages by Jennifer Lopez, Venus and Serena Williams, and Fergie to name a few, but the majority of ownership is by Stephen Ross. The Fins head coach is Joe Philbin who was a highly discussed person of interest league-wide last year, because the team was featured on the 2012 season of HBO's "Hard Knocks". The team isn't defined by the actions of former WR Chad Johnson (Ochocinco), so I'll discuss Philbin's role in his dismissal in the Scandals and Controversies section. A player who did define the Dolphins franchise was Dan Marino, who held every record in the league in passing, until Drew Brees of the Saints broke it in 2011. Marino was drafted by Miami in the first round of the 1983 draft, and retired with a passing record of 86.4 percent in 1999. The 1972 Miami Dolphins team is the only franchise in NFL history (pre-merger, and post), to go undefeated in regular season, plus the playoffs (17-0), and win the Super Bowl. The only other team to come close, was the 2007 New England Patriots, who finished the season perfect, but lost Super Bowl XLII to the New York Giants, 17-14.

The New England Patriots are considered one of the most successful teams in the league, primarily due to their win/loss ratio. Under head coach Bill Belichick (2000 – present in 2013), the Pats have put up 187 wins, to 101 losses, with Belichick's only losing season back in 2000, when the Pats finished 11-5, with a .313 winning percentage. The following season, they finished 11-5, first in the AFC East, and won Super Bowl XXXVI. The Patriots are largely operated by the Kraft family, owned by Robert Kraft, and play at Gillette Stadium in Foxborough, Massachusetts. The Patriots have accrued a stellar resume of three Super Bowls (2001, 2003, and 2004), seven AFC Championships, and numerous Playoff appearances. Of course, New York fans would want me to add that the Patriots have lost Super Bowls XLII (2007) and XLVI (2011) to the Giants. There are several key players for the organization which we've already discussed, including TE Rob

Gronkowski, but QB Tom Brady is imperative to know, because as of the 2012 season, the UGG model, and husband of Victoria's Secret model Giselle Bundchen, has thrown down an insane 44,806 passing yards, and 334 touchdowns since being drafted in the sixth round, 199th overall in the 2000 NFL Draft.

The New York Jets take heavy criticism yearly from the media for their off-the-field-antics, which includes, but isn't limited to head coach Rex Ryan's bizarre foot fetish, Antonio Cromartie's 12 children, and $500,000 child support loan, and throughout the 2012 season, The Tebow Chronicles – which seemingly overshadowed Ryan's outstanding weight loss, even. The Jets were originally called the Titans of New York, but during the merger, and as a result of new ownership, they were renamed and debuted into the NFL in 1970. The team operates out of East Rutherford, New Jersey, and holds a unique arrangement with the New York Giants, who share MetLife Stadium. The team is currently owned by Woody Johnson (Johnson & Johnson), who purchased the franchise in 1999 after the passing of Leon Hess. After a decade of four playoff appearances, and only one division championship, Johnson hired Rex Ryan in 2009, and showed promise by taking the team to the playoffs in 2009, and 2010.

AFC – North:

The Baltimore Ravens came to be as a result of former Cleveland Browns owner, Art Modell's decision to move his team to Baltimore by 1996. The relocation was a complete shitstorm of settlements, complications, and mediation, but it basically went like this: Modell wanted an entirely new team, but wanted to retain the Browns legacy, so a period of deactivation was issued from '96-'99, allowing him the NFL's 31st franchise. There was a provisional stipulation by the league, that if there were ever to be another divisional realignment, the Browns would share it with the Steelers, Ravens, and the Bengals – which happened in 2002. The Ravens (named after a poem by Edgar Allen Poe), currently play at M&T Bank Stadium, are owned by Steve Bisciotti, and are led by head coach John Harbaugh. They've won Super Bowl XXXV 34-7 against the Giants, and Super Bowl XLVII in 2012 against the San Francisco 49ers (34-31), and have been to the playoffs nine times.

The Cincinnati Bengals were a member of the AFL from 1968-1969, but became a member of the AFC conference as a result of the merger in 1970. Due to the realignment previously discussed with Baltimore, the Bengals became a member of the AFC North in 2002. They operate out of Cincinnati Ohio's Paul Brown Stadium, and are owned by Mike Brown, who takes on a lot of criticism yearly for how he "manages" the team and operations, with equal criticism given to head coach Marvin Lewis for his winning percentage (although, 2013 looks promising). Despite the Bengals' 11 playoff appearances, they've only won their post-realignment division twice (2005, 2009), and have lost their only Super Bowl appearances (two) to the 49ers.

The Cleveland Browns were established in 1946, but after a slew of integrations, and realignments (previously discussed), have been a member of the AFC-North since 2002. When people think of the Browns, "champion" isn't exactly the first word that comes to mind, but the Browns were hugely instrumental in establishing the modern game of football (post merger), and despite their winning percentage as of the past decade, they've seen a total of 28 playoff appearances, 11 conference championships, and four NFL Championships. The Browns play at Cleveland Browns Stadium, and are currently coached by Rob Chudzinski. Randy Lerner sold the franchise to Jimmy Haslam, which was approved of early in the 2012 season. Former players that should be known are Jim Brown, Brian Sipe, and Bernie Kolsar.

The Pittsburgh Steelers were established in 1933, and again, like the other teams minus Baltimore, became a member of the AFC-North as a result of the realignment in 2002. The Steelers are a controversial team, because the majority of the modern day fines for late hits have been imposed on players in the franchise, which is why people have dubbed it "Hittsburgh" (as opposed to the Bill Cowher coaching era of "Blitzburgh"). The Steelers play at Heinz Field, and have had the same owners since they were established: Art Rooney, and now, his son Dan Rooney. Since 2007, head coach Mike Tomlin has been at the helm, leading the team to two AFC Championships, and Super Bowl XLIII, where they edged the Arizona Cardinals 27-23. The current Steelers' roster includes some of the biggest names in the league, and with a defense made up of Troy Polamalu, Jarvis Jones, and Ike Taylor, it's easy to see why they have become such a defensively dominant team.

AFC – South:

The Houston Texans were established in 2001 by owners Bob McNair, and Harris County, Texas (five percent stake). Since their debut into the AFC South in 2002, they've called Reliant

Stadium home, which is a $455 million monstrosity I recommend everyone who passes through Texas see. While the Texans don't have the same deep seeded history as other teams, head coach Gary Kubiak (who is a Houston native) has seen the majority of the teams' progression since he arrived in 2006. For the Texans, 2011 was a statement year, as it was the first year they went to the playoffs, and their first AFC-South division championship; they repeated that feat again in 2012. The Texans roster is loaded with top-tier talent, but an important player in the books is Brian Cushing, who recorded the first safety for the Texans since 2002 against the Raiders on October 4, 2009 as a rookie. This, along with other plays resulted in Cushing winning the NFL Defensive Player of the Year award for that season – the second Texan to be awarded the DROY since DeMeco Ryans in 2006.

The Indianapolis Colts are one of those teams rich in history, and while Peyton Manning is now a Denver Bronco, time moved forward with Andrew Luck. The Colts were initially established in 1953 in Baltimore, Maryland, but moved to Indy in 1984, and became the fourth team in the AFC-South realignment in 2002. Jim Irsay took over sole ownership of the franchise after a legal battle with his mother after his father passed, and became the youngest NFL owner at 37. With a new franchise QB in Luck, Irsay had to hire a new head coach, so in the 2012 offseason, Chuck Pagano entered Indy ready to work. Since the realignment, the Colts have won their division seven times, and won Super Bowl XLI on February 4, 2007, 29-17 against the Chicago Bears. In total, the Colts have won two Super Bowls. Aside from Manning, other legends include Marvin Harrison, who put up 14,580 receiving yards from 1996-2008, and former head coach Tony Dungy, who not only had 85 wins with the franchise from 2002-2008, but has become an analyst, and highly motivating author, and philanthropist since. The Colts play at Lucas Oil Stadium, which has hosted Super Bowl's, a few NCAA Men's Basketball Finals, and is also home to the NFL Scouting Combine. Pagano was diagnosed with leukemia in week four of the 2012 season, and at Pagano's request, offensive coordinator Bruce Arians stepped up as the interim head coach. After three months of intensive treatment, it was announced that Pagano was in remission, and returned to his coaching duties on December 24th. If you see the words "Chuck Strong" anywhere, that's why.

The Jacksonville Jaguars joined the NFL as an expansion team in 1995, and play at EverBank Field. They are owned by Shahid Khan, a University of Illinois alum, and coached by Gus Bradley. The Jaguars were a product of an overwhelming lust for an NFL franchise by Jacksonville residents, who's only real source of football came every fall during the Gator Bowl between NCAA-F SEC rivals, the Georgia Bulldogs, and the Florida Gators. The team has gone to the playoffs six times, with no post-realignment AFC division championships, and no Super Bowl appearances.

The Tennessee Titans were originally established in 1959 as the Houston Oilers, but relocated to Nashville, Tennessee, and during the realignment in 2002, the Oilers moved from the AFC Central to the AFC-South. The team was already moved into their new house, LP Stadium by 1999, which is also when they assumed their new name, The Titans. The franchise is owned by Bud Adams, and coached by Mike Munchak, who played for the Oilers from 1982-1993. Post-realignment, the Titans have won two division championships, and have had 16 playoff appearances since the merger in 1972. A name that comes up often enough to discuss is Steve McNair, a former first round draft pick by the Oilers in 1995, and an NFL MVP award winner in 2003, with a QB rating of 82.8 percent. Unfortunately, McNair was shot four times, and killed on July 4, 2009 in a murder-suicide by his girlfriend, Sahel Kazemi.

AFC – West:

The Denver Broncos were established in 1960, and became part of the AFC-West in 1970. The Broncos play at Sports Authority Field at Mile High Stadium, and are owned by Pat Bowlen, with legendary former Broncos' QB John Elway as their General Manager, and are coached by John Fox. The Broncos, currently led by Peyton Manning, are one of the more successful franchises, winning two back-to-back Super Bowls under Elway (XXXII in 1997, 31-24 over the Green Bay Packers, and XXXIII in 2008, 34-19 over the Atlanta Falcons), with 12 division championships, and 19 playoff appearances. Notable players who have worn the navy and orange are Jay Cutler (now with Chicago) and Elvis Dumervil (Ravens).

The Kansas City Chiefs were originally called the Dallas Texans, but relocated to Kansas City in 1963 and joined the NFL during the merger. They became a member of the AFC-West in 1970, and moved into Arrowhead Stadium in 1972. The Chiefs are owned by the Hunt Family, and are coached by former Eagles' head coach, Andy Reid who replaced Romeo Crennel. While the Chiefs have never been to a Super Bowl, they have won their division six times since the merger, with 12 playoff appearances. Something nobody likes to bring up, but must be discussed, was the horrible murder-suicide by former Chiefs' linebacker Jovan

Belcher. On December 2, 2012, Belcher, 25, shot and killed his girlfriend Kasandra Perkins, who was the mother of their three-month-old daughter, then drove to Arrowhead Stadium, and shot himself in the head in the parking lot in front of Crennel, and general manager Scott Pioli, after thanking them for the opportunity (to play). The only information police were able to factor into the investigation as a possible motive, was that the couple had been having frequent arguments around the time of the incident.

The Oakland Raiders were established in 1960 as an AFL team, and became a member of the NFL during the merger. They joined the AFC-West in 1970 when they were still in Oakland, but from 1982-1994, they shared the field with the USC Trojans at the Los Angeles Memorial Coliseum. Al Davis moved the Raiders back to Oakland in 1995, where they currently play at the O. Co. Coliseum. Since the passing of Al Davis on October 8, 2011, his son Mark Davis, and Al's widow, Carol Davis inherited a 47 percent ownership, with majority controlling interest. The Raiders have won Super Bowls XI (1976, 32-14 against the Minnesota Vikings), XV (1980, 27-10 against the Philadelphia Eagles), and XVIII (1983, 38-9 against the Washington Redskins), with 12 AFC-West division championships, and 18 playoffs since 1970. The team is currently coached by Dennis Allen. Unfortunately, even the biggest fans see their current QB situation as a mess, but none compare to their former first round, first overall, 2007 draft pick out of LSU, Jamarcus Russell. Russell showed up in 2010 for offseason workouts overweight and out of shape, that ultimately led to his release. Russell was arrested on July 5, 2010 for possession of codeine syrup without a prescription, and analysts predicted that his "Purple Drank" legal battle would be his finale – they were right, making him one of the biggest draft busts in history; although Russell vows to return, eventually.

The San Diego Chargers were established in 1960, and became members of the AFC-West in 1970. They play at Qualcomm Stadium, which is owned by the City of San Diego, and are the only NFL team in Southern California. The Chargers are owned by Alex Spanos, and coached by Mike McCoy, who replaced Norv Turner (fired following the 2012 season) after failing to lead the franchise to a division win, or playoff game since 2009. During the 2011 Broncos/Chargers game on November 27, fans in the stadium went from screaming "Tebow Sucks!" to "Turner Sucks!" after the second half. The Broncos defeated the Chargers, 16-13 in OT that day, which should be an indicator of how much SD fans wanted him gone. With that said, despite 10 division championships, and 12 playoffs, the Chargers have never won a Super Bowl. Much like the other teams in this division, a list of high caliber athletes has inhabited San Diego at one point, including Drew Brees. Other notable former players include LaDanian Tomlinson, Vincent Jackson, Antonio Gates, Doug Flutie, and the late Junior Seau, who tragically committed suicide at 43 years old on May 2, 2012.

The NFC

Here is a breakdown of all 16 NFC teams by division, with brief background notes:

NFC – East: Dallas Cowboys, New York Giants, Philadelphia Eagles, and Washington Redskins.

NFC – North: Chicago Bears, Detroit Lions, Green Bay Packers, and Minnesota Vikings.

NFC – South: Atlanta Falcons, Carolina Panthers, New Orleans Saints, and Tampa Bay Buccaneers,

NFC – West: Arizona Cardinals, St. Louis Rams, San Francisco 49ers, and Seattle Seahawks.

NFC – East:

The Dallas Cowboys debuted in the NFL in 1960, but joined the NFC-East in 1970. Their stadium is in Arlington, Texas, and like the Texans, I highly suggest visiting AT&T Stadium if you're ever in the Dallas area; it truly is a magnificent modern marvel. Jerry Jones is the owner, president and general manager, and has been the focal point to the franchise since he purchased it in 1989. Jason Garrett, who hasn't yet taken them to a division title, coaches the Cowboys, but he's only been at the helm since 2010, after Jones fired then head coach, Wade Philips. Since 1970, the Cowboys have won 18 division championships, with 26 playoff appearances, and five Super Bowl Championships: VI (1971, 24-3 against the Miami Dolphins), XII (1977, 27-10 against the Denver Broncos), XXVII (1992, 52-17 against the

Buffalo Bills), XXXVII (1993, 30-13 against the Buffalo Bills), and XXX (1995, 27-17 against the Pittsburgh Steelers). Cowboys' Hall of Famers include (but aren't limited to): Tom Landry, Emmitt Smith, Michael Irvin, Troy Aikman, Tex Shchramm, and Tony Dorsett.

The New York Giants are one of the oldest teams in the league, and were established in 1925, but joined the NFC-East in 1970. Including pre-merger titles, the Giants rank third in the league with eight championships. Post-merger Super Bowl wins include XXI (1986, 39-20 against the Denver Broncos), XXV (1990, 20-19 against the Buffalo Bills), XLII (2007, 17-14 against the New England Patriots), and XLVI (2011, 21-17 against the New England Patriots, again). If you hadn't guessed by now, yes, the Giants and Patriots have a very strong cross-conference rivalry. The Giants are co-owned with a 50/50 split by John Mara and Steve Tisch, who also preside over the franchise. The G-Men have been coached by Tom Coughlin since 2004, who is a three-time Super Bowl champ himself, and has led the Giants to two Super Bowls, winning both.

The Philadelphia Eagles were established in 1933 and like most teams, they made the rounds until realignment landed them in the NFC-East in 1970. The Eagles play at Lincoln Financial Field and are owned by Jeff Lurie, who purchased the franchise in 1994. Andy Reid coached the Eagles from 1999-2012, and led them to an NFC Championship in 2004, but former Oregon Ducks head coach, Chip Kelly, replaced Reid in 2013. Since the realignment in 1970, the Eagles haven't won any Super Bowl Championships, but have eight division championships – six under Reid, and 19 playoff appearances. Eagles' Hall of Famers who you should know, are Mike Ditka, Sonny Jurgensen, Reggie White, Norm Van Brocklin, and Richard Dent. When Jurgensen played with the Redskins, he was fined $500 for saying "The only difference between Otto (Graham) and me, is that he likes candy bars and milkshakes, and I like women and scotch."

The Washington Redskins were established in 1932, but like the others in this division, joined the NFC-East in 1970. They play at FedEx Field in Landover, Maryland, which is a $383 million facility owned by 'Skins owner, Dan Snyder, who is partnered on the franchise with Dwight Schar, and Frederick Smith. The 'Skins are coached by Mike Shanahan, and have been to the playoffs 17 times, with seven division championships, five conference championships, and three Super Bowl wins, in XVII (1982, 27-17 against the Miami Dolphins), XXII (1987, 42-10 against the Denver Broncos), XXVI (1991, 37-24 against the Buffalo Bills), since the realignment. The most notable Hall of Famer is QB Joe Thiesmann who threw for 25,206-yards from 1974-1985 (and also had his career ended on a sack by Lawrence Taylor on November 18, 1985, that resulted in a compound fracture of his leg). Others include, Deion Sanders, Otto Graham, and Vince Lombardi.

NFC – North:

The Chicago Bears were established in 1919, but made their way into the NFC-North in 2002, along with the Lions, Packers, and Vikings. They play at Soldier Field in Chicago, Illinois, and are owned by Virginia McCaskey. In the entire history of the franchise, they've gone to the playoffs 25 times, with 18 division championships, and nine league championships. Since the realignment, they've won one conference championship, and three division championships, with three playoff appearances, that happened as a result of Lovie Smith taking over the head coaching position in 2004. The Bears' only Super Bowl win was XX in 1985, when they defeated the New England Patriots at the New Orleans Superdome, 46-10. Following the 2012 season, Lovie Smith was fired, and CFL – Montreal Allouettes coach, Marc Trestman was hired. While it was historically adapted through generations, the Bears are nicknamed "The Monsters of the Midway" because of the Bears' defense in 1985, who were ranked No.1 overall in points and yards allowed. The 1985 Bears went 15-1 in regular season, and went on to win Super Bowl XX, 46-10 on January 26, 1986 against the New England Patriots at the Louisiana Superdome in New Orleans, Louisiana.

The Detroit Lions were established in 1929, and became a member of the NFC-North in 2002. They are owned by William Ford Sr., and coached by Jim Schwartz, who has been at the helm since 2009. Since the Lions started playing at Ford Field in 2002, they've only had one playoff appearance, and that was in 2011. While they have yet to win a Super Bowl, they've been to the playoffs a total of 15 times, with four division championships since 1935. Some myth and folklore behind the Lions that I find amusing (although Lions fans find it terrifying), is that in 1958 Bobby Layne, a QB and PK, was traded to the Steelers. Layne allegedly said the Lions wouldn't win for 50 years in response to this trade, but as you can see from the less-than-stellar numbers above, the Lions haven't really fared so well, and haven't posted a championship since 1957. To make matters worse, throughout the years, Lions personnel have had several off-the-field issues, with arrests from President Tom Lewand's arrest on suspicion of

DUI in 2010, to Aaron Berry, who was released in July of 2012 upon his second arrest in that offseason alone.

The Green Bay Packers were established in 1919, in Green Bay Wisconsin, by Earl Lambeau, and had several affiliations before becoming a member of the NFC-North in 2002. The Packers have an interesting ownership, as it is made up of more than 112,000 shareholders, and is the only sports franchise in the United States that is owned solely *by* its shareholders. Mike McCarthy has coached the Packers since 2006, and has had much success, including the franchises second Super Bowl victory in 2010 (XLV) over the Steelers, 31-25. Packers' championships include another Super Bowl Victory under Mike Holmgren in 1997, where they defeated the Patriots, 35-21. They have a total of nine conference championships, three as an NFC team, 15 divisional championships – five in the NFC-North, and seven playoff appearances since the conference realignment. While the name "Lambeau" has so much history within the league, there is no greater place than Lambeau Field to see the history in its truest form. Much like the franchise ownership, Titletown USA is owned by the city of Green Bay, with an astonishing season ticket waitlist of 900 years! A common thing you will hear from any announcer covering a GB game is the "Lambeau Leap", which is when a Packer player jumps into the endzone crowd after a scoring play.

The Minnesota Vikings were established in 1961, and you guessed it, realigned in 2002 with the other three teams in the NFC-North. The Vikings are owned by Zigi Wilf, and coached by Leslie Frazier, who is going on his second season in 2013. The Vikings achieved success early in the franchise's history, having won the NFL Championship in 1969, and have been to the playoffs 25 times since the merger. Since the realignment, the Vikings have won two division championships (2008, 2009), with four playoff appearances (of 26, since 1968). Despite having promising talent, the Vikings seem to be plagued by QB issues yearly, and to add to the chaos, in 2010, the roof at the Hubert H. Humphrey Metrodome – home to the Vikings – collapsed due to an early December blizzard. Despite costing $18 million to fix the roof, the Vikings received approval to build a new stadium in May of 2012, which is expected to open by the 2016 season.

NFC – South:

The Atlanta Falcons were established in 1966, but joined the NFC-South during the realignment with the Panthers, Saints, and Bucs. The Dirty Birds have been to the playoffs 12 times, but since 2008, they've been knocked out in the first round. They won the NFC Conference in 1998 before the realignment, and the division in 2004, 2010, and 2012, where they posted a 13-3 record. Arthur Blank owns the franchise, with a slim portion by the State of Georgia. They are coached by Mike Smith, who has been at it since 2008, posting .700 in the regular season, and .200 in the post-season.

The Carolina Panthers were established in 1993 as an expansion team, and landed in the NFC-South in 2002. They are owned by Jerry Richardson, and over a dozen more people, and are coached by Ron Rivera who is going on his second season with the franchise in 2013. Since 2002, the Panthers have seen three playoffs, two division championships (2003, 2008), and one conference championship in 2003, where they went to Super

Bowl XXXVIII on February 1, 2004 in Houston, Texas, but lost 32-29 to the New England Patriots.

The New Orleans Saints are one of the most controversial and talked about franchise in the league for several reasons, mainly because the "Bountygate" investigation, which will be discussed in the Scandals and Controversies section. The Saints were established in 1967, and since joining the NFC-South in 2002, they've gone to the playoffs four times, winning the division three times, with a conference championship, and Super Bowl under their belt. Tom Benson (who purchased the New Orleans Pelicans {formerly Hornets} in 2012, as well) owns the Saints, and while Sean Payton was suspended for a year following Bountygate, Joe Vitt sat in as head coach for the majority of the 2012 season. Lots of things can be said about this historic team, such as Reggie Bush refusing to come to New Orleans if Payton drafted him in 2006, because NOLA and the Superdome were a disaster zone, due to being a place of refuge for those displaced during Hurricane Katrina in 2005. Well, obviously Reggie was drafted, and subsequently helped the Saints charge back from devastation to their first Super Bowl (XLIV) in 2009, when they defeated the Indianapolis Colts, 31-17 at Sun Life Stadium in Miami, giving QB Drew Brees the MVP Award. The Saints call the Mercedes Benz Superdome home, which cost $185 million to rebuild and renovate after Katrina.

The Tampa Bay Buccaneers – formerly called "The Yucks" – were established in 1976, and joined the division when it realigned in 2002. The Bucs play at Raymond James Stadium in Tampa, Florida, and are owned by Malcom Glazer, and managed by Mark Dominik, with second-year head coach Greg Schiano (formerly of Rutgers), who replaced Raheem Morris in 2012. In 2009, Morris' cuts and draft picks created a roster that orchestrated a 10-6, 2010 record. Unfortunately (conspiracy theories aside), the Bucs finished the 2011 season, 4-12, which resulted in the hiring of Schiano. Since 1979, the Bucs have posted 10 playoff appearances, and since realignment, three division championships, one conference championship, and won Super Bowl XXXVII, 48-21 against the Oakland Raiders on January 26, 2003 at Qualcomm Stadium in San Diego, CA. Aside from NFL badass Warren Sapp, former players and HOF'ers you should know from the Bucs are Steve Young, and Lee Roy Selmon, who passed on September 4, 2011 after suffering complications from a massive stroke.

NFC – West:

The Arizona Cardinals are the oldest team in the business, and were established in 1898. The Cardinals originated in Chicago, and are one of two, still-existing NFL charter members next to the Bears. Have you ever gotten the Arizona Cardinals mixed up with the St. Louis Cardinals? So did a lot of people, as the team was headquartered in St. Louis during the 60s and 70s. The Cards moved to Tempe, Arizona in 1988, and entered into the NFC-West during the realignment in 2002. They are owned by Bill Bidwell, and coached by Bruce Arians who replaced Kevin Wisenhunt after the 2012 season. Since 2006, the Cards have called University of Phoenix Stadium in Glendale, AZ home, which has been host to at-large college football games, such as the BCS National Championship, and the Fiesta Bowl, as well as Wrestlemania (WWE), and the host of Super Bowl XLII, when the Giants defeated the Patriots, 17-14 on February 3, 2008.

Since the realignment, the Cardinals have been to the playoffs, two times (eight total), with two division championships (2008, 2009), and despite having no Super Bowl wins of their own, they played in Super Bowl XLIII, but lost to the Steelers (27-23) at Raymond James Stadium in Tampa, FL on February 1, 2009. Kurt Warner is the most prolific player to suit up for the franchise, and in his four-year career (2005-2009) with the Cardinals, he lit up the single-season records. Another player that everyone should know about is Pat Tillman, who was a star linebacker at ASU, and was drafted in 1998 by the Cardinals. Tillman left the league and enlisted in the Army on May 31, 2002. On his second deployment to Afghanistan in 2004, Tillman was killed by friendly fire. The Cardinals have since retired No. 40, with Arizona State retiring his college number, 42. If you wish to donate or get involved with the Pat Tillman Foundation, please visit www.PatTillmanFoundation.com.

The St. Louis Rams were established in 1936 as the Cleveland Rams, and then spent 1946-1994 at the Los Angeles Memorial Coliseum playing as the Los Angeles Rams, before relocating to St. Louis in 1995. Despite their moves, the Rams have been a member of the NFC-West since 1970. Since then, they have been to the playoffs 19 times, with 11 division championships, three conference championships, and a Super Bowl championship (XXIV) on January 30, 1999 in a 23-16 win over the Titans. The franchise is owned by Stan Kroenke, and coached by Jeff Fisher, formerly of the Titans. Rams' Hall of Famers include RB Marshall Faulk, and Elroy Hirsch who played from 1949-1957 with 387 receptions for 7,029 yards and 60 TD's.

The San Francisco 49ers were established in 1946, and entered the NFC-West in 1970. If there is one thing you absolutely can't deny – even if you're a novice fan – is how awesome this franchise has been. People want to call the Cowboys "America's Team", but San Francisco has had the same number of Super Bowl wins: five, with XVI (January 24, 1982, in a 26-21 victory over the Bengals), XIX (January 20, 1985, 38-16 win over the Dolphins), XXIII (January 22, 1989, 20-16 win over the Bengals), XXIV (January 28, 1990, 55-10 win over the Broncos), and XXIX (January 29, 1995, 49-25 win over the Chargers). Despite being historically "off" by a year (as the Gold Rush boomed in 1948), the 49ers – who play at Candlestick Park on San Francisco's beautiful coastline (with a move to Santa Clara, CA scheduled for 2014)– are a team rich in history, from Bill Walsh, Joe Montana, Steve Young, Ronnie Lott, Richard Dent, and Jerry Rice. If you're ever in the market for a book to expand your knowledge on the 9ers franchise from inception by the DeBartolo family, through the modern day, I suggest *The Genius*, by David Harris. Jed York currently owns the 9ers, who are managed by Trent Baalke, and coached by Jim Harbaugh, who was hired out of Stanford after the 2010 season, to replace Mike Singletary, who posted a 5-10 record that year. Harbaugh instantly commanded the Faithful in his first season, by ending their nine-year playoff drought, and posting a regular season record of 13-3, charging all the way to the NFC Championship game, where they lost to the Giants. In 2012, Harbaugh, and starting QB Colin Kaepernick went to Super Bowl XLVII where they lost to the Ravens, 34-31.

The Seattle Seahawks joined the NFL in 1976, but realigned with the previous three teams in 2002, in the revamped NFC-West. The Seahawks have been mentioned throughout this book already, with how noise effects play (with CenturyLink

Field registering seismic activity against the Saints in the playoffs), to Marshawn Lynch and his Skittles. The Seahawks are owned by Paul Allen who co-founded Microsoft, and purchased the franchise in 1997. They are managed by John Schneider, and coached by former USC badass, Pete Carroll who took over in 2010. In his first three seasons in Seattle, Carroll won 25 games, with 23 losses. Since the realignment, the Seahawks have been to the playoffs seven times, with five division championships,

and one conference championship.

Hall Of Fame

The Hall of Fame was established in 1963, and is located in Canton, Ohio, where the game was founded. The purpose of the HOF, is to preserve and honor those who impacted the game whether on the field, or in the booth.

The selection committee is made up of 44 representatives from various outlets, including media, who vote on 17 finalists to be enshrined yearly, that are nominated by everyone from fans, to panelists.

The shrine features exhibits with artifacts from when football was born, to modern day apparel that have been donated by teams, or by the players themselves.

Hall of Fame week occurs during the first week of pre-season in August. The induction festivities happen during the week, with the Hall of Fame Game held that weekend to conclude the ceremonies, and kickoff pre-season. This tradition has been carried through the decades since it began on August 11,

1962, that resulted in a 21-apiece tie, between the Giants and Cardinals. The only time the game has been canceled in its 50-year history, was in 2011, which was due to the NFL Lockout, and fortunately, the only casualty of that labor war.

NFL Playoffs

So the season has come, and gone. August has turned into December, and now it's time to break out the brackets and slot your foreshadowed Super Bowl winner. But how are the playoff teams selected, and what's a "Wild Card"?

To expand on the explanation from several chapters back, of the 32 NFL teams, only 12 will make it to the playoffs, and that's based on eight division champions (four from the NFC, and four from the AFC), and a team from each division with the next best record, who qualify as Wild Cards. In the event of a tie breaker, the teams are compared on a matrix of 1st, 2nd, 3rd, and 4th best records in the division based on head-to-head divisional games, wins and losses within the division, win/loss percentages among games where common teams were played, win margins (scores), strength of schedules, net touchdowns, and other variables.

The first round are the AFC and NFC Wildcard games. The four winners (two AFC/two NFC) advance to the Divisional Playoff games, where the two winners from each move on to the AFC and NFC Championship games. The winners from each, then advance to the Super Bowl.

The Pro Bowl

Throughout this book, "Pro Bowlers" have been referenced several times, and these athletes are significant because from 1971 until 2012, they were voted upon by the fans and their peers, to represent their teams in an AFC, versus NFC game played in Hawaii, the week before the Super Bowl.

On July 31, 2013, the NFL and NFLPA released a statement discussing major changes to the Pro Bowl. For starters, there will no longer be an AFC versus NFC game; it is now an All-Star Game, where players will be assigned to teams through an NFL Pro Bowl Draft. Two NFL.com Fantasy Football champions, will join two other leading vote winners to create the teams, and Pro Football Hall of Famers, Jerry Rice and Deion Sanders will serve as alumni captains, where they will assist fantasy champions, and Pro Bowl team captains throughout the draft process.

The 2014 Pro Bowl Draft will be held on January 22, 2014, on NFL Network, with the game on January 26 in Hawaii, on NBC.

The rules are significantly different compared to a regular game, which fans despise, but the goal is to get drunk, act like an ass, and get paid for it; not graphically, or catastrophically hurt your opponents.

The differences in rules are: two-minute warnings for the first and third quarters, there are 43-man rosters (86 total), no kickoffs (will be placed at the 25-yard line after each scoring play, or start of new quarter), no blitzing (yawn), no rushing kickers or punters, defenses must run a 4-3 and are permitted to play cover-two, or press coverage. Intentional grounding is illegal (and punishable by Mai Tai's), with TE's required in all offensive formations, and a few others, but that's the gist.

In recent years, players have been trying to see how far the rules envelope can be pushed, by going rogue throughout the game. This is primarily because the athletes feel that in order to pull a thinning Pro Bowl fan-base back in, there needs to be more contact and normal procedures that fans love during the regular season, and the playoffs.

For athletes to put up with these shenanigans (and fans tweeting athletes: "I hate the Pro Bowl, you should have FINISHED HIM! THIS. IS. SPARTA!"), they are handsomely compensated with an all-expense paid vacation for them, as well as a $50,000 payout per player for a win, and $25,000 per player who loses. Not bad.

The Super Bowl

Most of us know what the Super Bowl is, but for the complete newcomer, it's the biggest game of the year, with the AFC Champion, and NFC Champion going head-to-head in primetime.

The very first Super Bowl was played on January 15, 1967, between the Green Bay Packers and the Kansas City Chiefs, at the Los Angeles Memorial Coliseum, where the Packers routed the Chiefs, 35-10.

The Steelers have won six, and lost two, with the 49ers in second place at five wins, one loss, and the Cowboys a close third at five wins, and three losses.

Teams without a Super Bowl win are the Vikings, Bills, Bengals, Eagles, Chargers, Falcons, Titans, Panthers, Seahawks, Cardinals, Browns, Lions, Jaguars, and the Texans. Of that list, there are four teams who have never even been to the Super Bowl: the Texans, Jaguars, Lions and Browns.

Every year we hear about Super Bowl commercials and how much those 30-second spots run from around $4 million, onwards of up to $6 million. The most infamous commercials in recent history came in 2010, with Tim Tebow and his mother Pam, who were scheduled to appear on behalf of conservatives, and the pro-life organization, Focus on the Family. The ad didn't mention abortion, but carried a strong message.

Another politically charged ad came in 2012, when Chrysler Motor Company ran an unprecedented two-minute ad discussing the rebound of Detroit and its automakers, which was a truly powerful and financially uplifting message for America. But conservatives saw it as an early re-election campaign start for President Obama's second term. This is ironic, because the commercial was narrated by Clint Eastwood, who endorsed 2012 Presidential Election, GOP candidate, Mitt Romney.

The Lombardi Trophy

The Vince Lombardi Trophy is the most highly sought after, and coveted trophy in football. The trophy is named after Vince Lombardi – who was the head coach of the Green Bay Packers, and led them to win the first two Super Bowl titles in 1966, and 1967.

The first production began in 1967, with a sketch by Tiffany & Co vice president, Oscar Riedner. Since then, Tiffany's has been the exclusive manufacturer of the 22-inch, seven-pound, $50,000 sterling silver trophy.

The Draft Process

This section is a brief 101 on the Draft process events:

- **Declaration**: When a player declares for the NFL Draft, he must have at least three years of secondary play in order to be eligible. When a player declares himself, he signs a contract with the league that basically means he is no longer an amateur, making him ineligible to return to play college ball. But there's a 3-day window for the athlete to change his mind.

- **The NFL Scouting Combine**: is when a player gets invited to Indy to perform drills, and interview with scouts from all 32 NFL teams. This is considered to be one of the biggest job interviews a person could ever be scheduled for, because not only does it test your mind through the Wonderlic exam, and interviews, it tests how fast you function in various skill-set position drills. Athletes receive their invitations in December of their last college season, after declaring themselves eligible for the draft. Not everyone receives an invitation, and certainly just because a guy receives one, doesn't guarantee that he'll get drafted. Regional Combines are are also held in various locations, where athletes who weren't invited to *the* Scouting Combine, can register in their last college season, to showcase their talent.

- **Tests Include**: the 40-yard dash, vertical jump, Wonderlic, drug evaluation, physicals, interviews, 60-yard shuttle, three-cone drill, broad jump, 20-yard shuttle, bench press (225 pounds, unlimited reps), and position specific drills, like running routs and blocking.

Pro Days happen in March, typically, and are basically a second in-person assessment for players who were invited to the Combine. For players who weren't invited, this gives them an opportunity to try out in front of scouts and impress them.

The NFL Draft

The NFL Draft is a three-day event, held at the Radio City Music Hall, in New York City in April every year; although it will be held May 8-10, in 2014. The Draft process can be confusing with the selection order, trades, compensatory picks, and number of selections overall, but here is a breakdown of all this event in its most simplified form:

- The Draft order is pretty much as follows: Shittiest to the best. Usually, the 20 teams that didn't go to the playoffs go first, with the Wild Card, Divisional, Conference Championship, Super Bowl loser, and then the Super Bowl winner, to round out the pecking order.

- Trades can throw a curveball into the order, and can never be predicted, as teams are not only vying the most qualified player on the boards for the positions they need filled, but they're up against 31 other teams who are potentially gunning for him, too. If a team goes into the Draft with nine selections, there's a reason for this; either they traded players for picks during the season, or they were acquired during the previous years' Draft from a team wanting to trade up to get a player. The more picks a team has going into a Draft, the more leverage it has.

- There are 32 Compensatory picks, and are given as

compensation to teams who lost more (or better) players than they were able to acquire during the Free Agency period (that begins in March). These picks are usually given to teams several weeks before the Draft, to help them better plan their hopeful Draft class more efficiently.

- The number of selections an individual team can have, varies on how many picks they come in with, and acquire during. There are seven rounds, with 32 selections per round, so that equals a total of 224 selections. Now with the Compensatory picks, that number goes up to 256.

- The 244th pick is always called "Mr. Irrelevant", and it doesn't mean anything; it's just a funny jab at the final pick.

The Supplemental Draft was created in 1977, as a way for teams to get after players who, for whatever reason, were unable to declare for the Draft in April. The Supplemental is usually held in July, and the most recent player to turn heads was in 2011, with former Ohio State QB, Terrelle Pryor, who (by way of agent extraordinaire Drew Rosenhaus) was selected by the Oakland Raiders.

Free Agency

Three types define these athletes: Undrafted Rookie Free Agent (or UDRFA/UDFA), Restricted Free Agent (RFA), or Unrestricted Free Agent (UFA). For a player to be a Restricted Free Agent, he must have three accrued seasons, and to be an Unrestricted Free Agent, he must have four accrued seasons, which means that he was either active/inactive, on injured reserve, or the physically unable to perform (PUP) list for six, or more regular season games. Teams are allowed to place a Franchise Tag on one unrestricted player every year, which is a 1-year deal, and pays the player 120 percent of the previous contract, and no less than the average of the top five players at that respective position, whichever is more.

- Undrafted Rookie Free Agents are rookies who went undrafted. It's that simple. Think of it like *The Bachelor*, or other dating shows. The UDFA's are all the contestants who didn't get picked.

- Restricted Free Agents are available to discuss interest with other teams, but in order for the existing team to hold onto the player, they must match what the interested team is offering. This transaction usually involves some draft picks as part of the negotiating terms. One way to look at this, is if you're still in a relationship, but you have the worlds worse wandering eye and are constantly interviewing for potential affairs, which could turn into relationships; just make sure he offers similar good qualities that your current possesses.

- Unrestricted Free Agents are players who aren't with teams by contract expiration, or release. As long as there are no contractual attachments binding a player to a team, he is free to roam about the country, and pick his next spot based off offers from teams. My favorite way of explaining this, is that if you're single, you're an Unrestricted Free Agent! Now, divorcees might have some baggage still, so if that's the case, you might want to check with your lawyers before putting yourselves back on the market. Officially.

Rosters

Several questions come up throughout the season, so this is a brief explanation on how to read rosters, practice squads, and differentiate between other terms regarding personnel, and injuries. These factors also explain why "Inactive" lists are so closely monitored by teams and fans, prior to the game starting.

- NFL teams are made up of 53 roster spots – with 47 who actually dress on game day. How the coaching staff and management want to allocate those positions is up to them, and there is no set position number requirement. For example, a franchise could enter camp with six quarterbacks, and end up with three by the time rosters are trimmed.

- Practice Squads are scout teams, and made up of eight members. They are usually paid league minimum, and are typically players that teams are in the bubble on, or just need more time to develop.

- Injured Reservists are players who can't play. When a player is transferred to IR, it means he's still on the team, but it allows the franchise the flexibility to add an alternative to maintain 53 players.

- There are two versions of Physically Unable to Perform (PUP): Pre-season PUP, which is when a player is injured during pre-season, and regular season PUP, which sidelines the player for six weeks. If a player who is put on pre-season PUP rolls over onto the regular season PUP, regular season rules apply. Those six weeks are spent with the player practicing during the first half, with the second half spent deciding whether to activate him, or keep him on the PUP list for the rest of the season.

Scandals, Controversies, and Issues

I interviewed former USC Trojans TE, Alex Homes (@Trojan81 on Twitter) during production of this book, because there were many issues I felt spectators from every level needed unfiltered responses to. The next few pages discuss everything from the importance of education, to a failed run in the league, and safety:

Here is the raw transcription from our interview, which should clarify some questions or concerns firsthand:

VF - So you went undrafted in 2005, and signed with the Miami Dolphins as a Free Agent. What was that process like?

AH - Difficult because I was the third highest ranked TE behind Heath Miller. I was invited to the Senior Bowl, and Combine, so it was weird not to get drafted. But even though I had never gotten in trouble, I had the reputation of being the party guy, and it hurt me. I should have known it then, but I was immature and I didn't realize it, or why, until years later.

I look back and I remember at the Senior Bowl and Combine, and I would sit down for my one-on-ones, and instead of asking about football for the first couple of minutes, they were just saying how I was the guy to call for entertainment... I just couldn't detach myself from the stigma of handling recruits I hosted on their visits at SC.

VF - Did you expect to get drafted? What were your overall expectations?

AH - I expected to be drafted. When I left SC I was an all-time TE receiver, and a really good blocking TE... I played really well at the Senior Bowl. Going out (partying) definitely hindered my stock.

~ The National Football League ~

VF - When you were waived from Miami, and then the Rams, how did the process go? Did they say something to the effect of "We're sorry, but we've gone in a different direction?

AH – I was waived from Miami because (Nick) Saban blamed me when Ricky Williams (multiple failed drug tests for marijuana, which forced a retirement until Williams returned to Miami in 2007) got in trouble. The Rams… yeah, they were standard release procedure.

VF - Do you think that coming from a university that stressed education helped you to adapt to the real world better after deciding that your football career was over?

AH – College Football is a business. I came from an educated family, and academics always played a part in everything I did, but CFB is a big money business, and 70 percent of those guys are just there to play football. For me, it's helped in business, and the networking I did at SC helps me every day.

VF - Compared to others in your situation, how do you think your life has fared after football?

AH – I've done well. I had a period of time when I had no idea what to do; I was depressed and upset… I hadn't come to terms with the fact that I wasn't going to play football anymore. It was rough, but other than that I was able to make the transition well.

VF - Your brother-in-law is Steelers SS Troy Polamalu, so based on your family ties and strong connections to the organization, what's your take on league fines for hits?

AH - It's ridiculous. Anywhere else, if you get fined there's an appeal process where a third-party makes the decision. In the NFL, it goes back to the guy who initially fines you. The same goes with the appeal process. It's just wrong. If they're going to fine guys, they should fine the teams. Guys have to be responsible for their actions, but the league needs to fine teams evenly. Football is a brutal game and people are going to get hurt. There's a sense that it's being taken away.

VF - What's your take on the safety issues?

AH - I think they're doing more than enough, but the bottom line is that football is violent and dangerous; players are bigger, stronger and faster. In the 70s nobody ran a 4.3 (40) at 270 pounds, so the game is evolving, and its nice to make the game safer, but I'd like to see a big jump in the technology for the gear.

VF - After playing football all your life, what are the most common post-career issues a former player's body goes through?

AH - I personally broke my back, broke my shoulder, had reconstructive surgery on that… I feel like a 50-year-old man, but that's pretty common. There are things that you worry about with mental stuff. I never had a concussion, but my short-term memory isn't that great. I hit people with my head for years, and years, but that's really it.

Miami 2012:

Six-time Pro Bowler, Chad Johnson (Ochocinco) was released from the Miami Dolphins on August 12, 2012, a day after being arrested for allegedly "head butting" his wife of six weeks, Basketball Wives star, Evelyn Lozada. The two got into verbal altercation after Lozada allegedly found the receipt for a box of condoms in Johnson's car. When police arrived, she had a gash on her forehead.

Lozada filed for divorce the next day, after Johnson was released on a $2,500 bail, however, as sponsors dropped him, his future career was deemed questionable – at best.

Johnson continued to train during the 2012 season, but never made a roster. In June 2013, Johnson was sentenced to spend 30-days in jail after slapping his attorneys ass in front of the judge during his plea-bargaining, but was released days later.

New Orleans Saints Bountygate:

Bountygate was the result of a two-year investigation by the League, after opponents of the New Orleans Saints defense reported to the NFL that several hits were deliberate. To make a long story short, the league ruled that players on the Saints D – including defensive coordinator, Gregg Williams – had a slush fund that paid out large sums of cash for bounties that were carried out on their opponents. As a result of this investigation, on March 21, 2012 Commissioner Goodell handed the following sanctions to the Saints:

- *A $500,000 fine.*
- *The loss of second round Draft picks in 2012, and 2013.*
- *The suspension of Gregg Williams until the end of the 2012 season.*
- *The suspension of HC Sean Payton for the 2012 season, with no possibility of reinstatement until April 1, 2013 (no, this was not an April Fools Day joke.)*
- *And the suspension of GM Mickey Loomis for the first half of the 2012 season.*

Several players were suspended for their role in Bountygate, including Scott Fujita (three games, now with the Browns), Anthony Hargrove (eight games/ Packers), Saints DE Will Smith (four games), and LB Jonathan Vilma – who was suspended for the entire 2012 season.

The NFLPA (NFL Players' Union) filed a federal lawsuit and appeal, on behalf of the players suspended that challenged Goodell's ruling, claiming it was out of his jurisdiction. Goodell responsibly recused (dismissed) himself of presiding over the appeal, and appointed former NFL commissioner Paul Tagliabue to oversee and hear the appeal. In September 2012, the Players Union won a unanimous decision in the players' favor, claiming it was a violation of the Collective Bargaining Agreement, and didn't give Goodell the authority to issue the punishment. The NFL offered to reduce the suspensions if Vilma agreed to drop his defamation suit against the NFL, and Goodell. He didn't.

On December 11, 2012, Tagliabue issued his final decision, declaring that the suspensions, fines, and loss of draft picks were to be upheld, citing, "Goodell's findings and the resulting suspensions of these Saints' personnel are final and no longer subject of appeal. I affirm commissioner Goodell's factual findings as to the four players."

Tagliabue decided on several distinct findings on each member involved, which ultimately were the reasons he upheld the rulings. Disciplinary actions against all four players were vacated, lifting two of the games left in Hargrove's decision, and vacating Fujita's, Vilma's and Smith's suspensions.

Tagliabue did, however, find Vilma's actions and conduct to be "detrimental to the integrity of, and public confidence in, the game of professional football", as there was sufficient evidence through a speech in 2010, where he allegedly offered a $10,000 bounty to any player who hurt former Vikings' QB Brett Favre.

On January 17, 2013, Judge Helen Berrigan, a New Orleans federal judge, dismissed Vilma's defamation suit against Goodell. Berrigan found that Vilma's claim was insufficient, and that Goodell was within the jurisdiction of the CBA. Berrigan also slammed Goodell for neglecting due process and players' rights, claiming the investigation was "procedurally flawed", despite having "enough support to defeat the defamation claims."

Titus Young:

As of May 2013, the most notable arrest was former Detroit Lions' wide receiver Titus Young, who was arrested on a DUI, then arrested again within 15 hours, trying to break into the impound lot to get his vehicle. He was arrested again that same week, for breaking into a home, then on second-degree commercial burglary after allegedly stealing items from a Chevron store. Young was a Free Agent at the time, but it certainly didn't help his hiring process, and many speculated that this behavior is why he, and the Rams parted ways after a 10-day contract in February 2013.

Young's father, Richard, said that he believed the string of incidents were attributed to a concussion, and that Young was prescribed anti-psychotics to combat mental issues.

Aaron Hernandez:

On June 26, 2013, former Patriots tight end Aaron Hernandez, 23, was charged with the murder of semi-professional football player for the Boston Bandits, Odin Lloyd, 27, who's body was found near Hernandez' Attleboro, Massachusetts home, with keys to a vehicle rented under Hernandez' name.

According to the District Attorney, Lloyd was shot with a .45 caliber Glock multiple times, in his chest (heart), arm, side, groin, and back, on June 17, 2013.

Hernandez allegedly destroyed his home surveillance system, along with his cell phone, and other pieces of evidence, including up to eight hours of footage on the surveillance tape.

Hernandez was taken into custody on the morning of Wednesday, June 26, 2013, shortly after the Patriots released him from the team, where he was arraigned on charges of murder in the first degree, and five counts of firearms possession, including illegal weapons charges, and plead not-guilty on all counts.

Allegedly, the initial motive for the murder was that Lloyd had engaged in conversation with a group of people that Hernandez had issues with, at a nightclub several days prior to the murder. However, prosecutors said it could also be related to what Lloyd know about a double homicide in Boston in 2012.

The prosecutor alleges that Hernandez and two associates, Carlos Ortiz, 27, of Bristol, Conn., and Ernest Wallace, 47, of Miramar, Fla. (who waived his right to contest extradition - and returned to Massachusetts to face accessory to murder charges), entered a convenience store to purchase gum and cigars, but a piece of the gum matching the brand purchased was recovered in the rental vehicle, along with a shell casing matching the .45 caliber bullet used in the murder.

When 156 pages of court documents were unsealed on July 9, 2013, it was revealed that Wallace allegedly told Ortiz that Hernandez was the shooter. After his arrest, Ortiz informed law enforcement about an apartment in Franklin, Massachusetts that was rented in Hernandez's name. Inside, they recovered Ortiz' cell phone (that Ortiz told them was there), along with several boxes of ammunition, where a fingerprint matching

Hernandez was also found. A Hummer belonging to Hernandez was recovered at the apartment complex, with a loaded .45 caliber clip hidden inside. During arraignment, the prosecutor said that Hernandez "orchestrated the execution" (of Lloyd), and requested he be held without bail, which the judge agreed upon.

At the time *The Modern Girl's Guide to the Gridiron* went to print, this case and investigation was onging, the murder weapon hadn't been found, and other murders alleging Hernandez' involvement were also being investigated.

In any event where an athlete is troubled, it's best to let the courts and due process decide their punishment, and as spectators and fans, it should be our responsibility to wish them well in instances where alcohol or substance abuse, and neurological issues disrupt their lives, and hope they get help. And in cases similar to Hernandez's, hope the justice system gets it right.

Badgering, harassing, or berating an athlete will not help them in their process to stable, overall mental health, and as we've seen time after time, athletes or celebrities who don't get help, only become volcanoes waiting to erupt.

The Madden Curse

The Madden Curse is said to happen when the athlete who appears on the cover of the video game "Madden", and gets injured the following season. While it's an honor to have your face on the cover of the EA game, players from Michael Vick, Peyton Hillis, Donovan McNabb, and Brett Favre have experienced this curse.

This is why you will see or hear athletes campaigning for this honor, saying that they will beat the curse. It happens year after year, but until someone who lands on the cover, goes on to win a Super Bowl the following year without injury, you should be a little skeptical, too.

Marijuana, per 2012 Presidential/General Election Results

While several states approved of the use of medicinal marijuana (with Colorado voting in favor of an all-around legalization), the NFL, and NCAA have still listed marijuana as a banned substance, regardless of state laws.

Don't be an idiot, and abide by rules to which athletes are under contract, and please spread this public service announcement to anyone who has contact with athletes. Trust me when I say that college and professional athletes have, and will continue to be suspended or waived for the usage of illegal substances. The risk is not worth the ensuing repercussions.

It is also important for wives, girlfriends, or associates of athletes to know what drugs are illegal, and know what the side affects, and long-term results could be.

~ The National Football League ~

International Football

There are several forms of International Football, but the main ones that always fall into discussion are NFL London, and the Canadian Football League.

NFL London is referred to as the International Series, and since 2007, the series has been played at London's Wembley Stadium. Teams who agree to play across the pond, do so with the stipulation that they have to give up one home game that season.

Mexico City:

- October 2, 2005 – The Cardinals beat the 49ers, 31-14 in Mexico City.

At Wembley:

- October 28, 2007 – The Giants beat the Dolphins 13-10.
- October 26, 2008 – The Saints beat the Chargers 37-32.
- October 25, 2009 – The Patriots beat the Bucs 35-7.
- October 31, 2010 – The 49ers beat the Broncos 24-16.
- October 23, 2011 – The Bears beat the Bucs 24-18.
- October 28, 2012 – The Patriots beat the Rams 45-7.

Chapter Six
The Canadian Football League

The Canadian Football League gets a lot of attention in the United States, because the CFL teams feature a lot of former American players and prospective talents for future NFL rosters. The CFL is also over 100 years old.

The CFL is made up of 8 teams: the Hamilton Tiger-Cats, Montreal Alouettes, Toronto Argonauts, Saskatchewan RoughRiders, Winnipeg Blue Bombers, Edmonton Eskimos, Calgary Stampeders, and the British Columbia Lions.

The league experimented with an American expansion that failed, and now its focusing on expanding in Canada, and adding a ninth team for 2014.

Pre-Season starts in June, with kickoff on Canada Day Weekend (July 1) to start a 19-week, 18-game regular season that ends at the beginning of November. Six of the eight teams will head to the seeded semi-final playoffs, where the winners of those two games advance to play in the Grey Cup – its version of the Super Bowl.

One of the biggest differences between the CFL and NFL, is that each CFL roster is limited to 42 players who dress, on a 46-man active roster, that includes a maximum of 20 non-Canadian (or Import) players. It's important to mention that quarterbacks are almost always American players.

~ The Canadian Football League ~

A friend of mine, John Bender (@JohnW_Bender on Twitter), a Three Hills, Alberta, Canada native, was drafted in 2011, in the third round with the 17th pick by the Calgary Stampeders, so I went to him for a no-holds-barred inside angle on how the CFL compares to the NFL:

"The CFL is a very different brand of football. The three down formats along with several other rules changes make it a very different game. It's interesting to see how some players like Ricky Williams can be NFL greats, yet his one season in the CFL was very average. Mobile QB's who can get out of the pocket, yet are still very accurate, and maybe a little bit undersized such as Doug Flutie and Jeff Garcia have shown to be very productive in both leagues. Warren Moon as well, as he's the only player to be in both the CFL, and NFL Hall of Fame.

The CFL is a great league for younger players who have no other options left to play. Arena football doesn't pay as well as the CFL does, and we all know that NFL Europe no longer exists and the UFL is all but over. The CFL is also a great league for players who maybe don't have the prototypical body type the NFL is looking for.

One of the greatest receivers in the CFL today, and Perennial Most Outstanding Player Candidate (CFL's version of the MVP) is Nik Lewis. He's generously listed around 5'11 (though, closer to 5'9") and he weighs around 240 pounds. That screams NFL fullback or linebacker. He consistently catches around 100 passes and punishes the smaller linebackers and defensive backs trying to tackle him.

Comparatively to NFL numbers, the CFL is able to get players at a very cheap rate. Around $45-50,000/year is what entry-level contracts usually look like. Keep in mind, six of the eight teams get playoff bonus money, which is substantial, and Grey Cup Champions receive almost $25,000 in bonus pay. Once you establish yourself in this league, you can make well over $100,000/year. But with small roster sizes of 42 players dressing each game, and only eight teams. Competition is fierce. There isn't much room for back-ups, and most players who start also play special teams. With 12 starters on each side of the football, plus three downs, means special teams play a bigger role in the game. If you come up to the CFL and you're good, you're playing one way or another. Or, you're on the practice roster making a very slim salary of $500/week with your living expenses covered. Only six offensive linemen dress for each game, and typically four, or more of the six are Canadian.

What most players like about the CFL is the opportunity. There are guys on teams who never went to college, or only played at the JC level. Right beside them, are players like Noel Devine, Chris Leak, Mitch Mustain, and other NCAA stars. Players who were highly sought after college recruits and NCAA players, are right beside a guy like Nik Lewis, and Rob Cote who I went to high school with in Cochrane, AB, who started playing with the Stampeders at the age of 20, having never playing University football. Rob is now a seven year CFL Veteran.

It was interesting to see how many players I played against in college, like Chris Williams and JC Sherritt of Eastern Washington University. They are two of the best players in the CFL now, and I remember thinking in college, "these guys can play, they're just too small to play in the NFL." Sheritt won an award last year, and so did Williams – I believe.

In the CFL, with the larger field and different game, these guys are dominant. They're probably playing for around league minimum salary, and they will continue to improve, and may take a shot at the NFL one day like Doug Flutie did, and never look back. Or, they could take the road of a guy like Anthony Calvillo, or Ricky Ray from Sacramento State (who won the Grey Cup last year with Toronto) and be a CFL superstar, and play until he's 40 making around NFL minimum salary every year. $300-400K/year. He probably makes a little more than that, though.

It's a different league with a different mentality. I can't tell you

~ The Canadian Football League ~

how many former Stampeders are millionaires in the business community in Calgary now; it's a lot, probably over a dozen. It's a great opportunity to build your name, your network, and your net-worth. Most CFL players work another job. Even during the season. Under CFLPA rules, they are only allowed to keep players there for five hours/day, typically from 8am-1pm.

Some players use the free time to work as financial advisors, real estate agents, bankers, or car salesmen to supplement income for them, and their families. Some players use the time to chase women and play video games. It's all a decision making process, like anything else. There are opportunities everywhere you look to be successful, both during, and after your football career. It's up to players to seek out those opportunities. It's much different than everything I've heard about the NFL from former (Nevada) teammates, where workdays can be from 7am, until 5-6pm, on almost a daily basis, with no real opportunities, or desires to work another job at the same time. It's unique. These players are given an opportunity to succeed, and they try to take full advantage of it. It's really all they ask for."

Chapter Seven
The Media

Sideline Reporters

Sideline Reporters were introduced in 1974 by ABC, as the final touch to the reporting trifecta; which includes play-by-play analysts and color commentators, who typically assist in the broadcast and analysis, with random facts and stories.

I hope you're still fired up about the "Inez Sainz' ass" reference from the beginning of the book, but most reporters do a good job, *doing their job* of reporting the news and chasing coaches down the sideline for a story, or a one-liner.

The majority of the sideline analysis is loaded with great information, but I never had aspirations of being a sideliner because I always felt the job was a bit intrusive. For example, say you're a coach and your team is down 24-points at the half. While you're racing to rally your soldiers, the last thing you want to deal with are reporters, and the repetitive, menacing barrage of questioning such as: "So Coach, what are you planning on doing to change (insert issue here) in the second half?"

While it's all smiles for the most part, catching a coach when he's in the zone and on his way to the locker room can be terrifying, so if you want an idea, look up "John L. Smith's meltdown against Ohio State in 2005" by AnnArborIsAWhore on YouTube.

For years on college game days, we focused our attention on the blond-haired University of Florida Gator duo, Erin Andrews, and Jenn Brown who graced the sidelines, interviewing coaches from Pete Carroll, Mack Brown, Tim Tressel to Urban Meyer. But there are so many more we should be able to identify, such as Alex Flanagan (NFL Network, NBC Sports, and Football Night in America), Samantha Steele Ponder (ESPN and The Longhorn Network), and Wendi Nix (ESPN).

Notable sideliner reporters for the NFL that you should know of, are Emmy award winning pioneer Michele Tafoya, Jenn Brown (NFL Network), and Tracy Wolfson with NFL on CBS covering pre, and post season.

Whether they annoy you, or make the game more personable for you, the truth behind the lady personnel on the sidelines, are that they're generally very well educated women, who have to work ten-times harder just to get the advantage, so respect is definitely due.

Football Analysts

Every Saturday, millions upon millions of fans, turn their flat screens on to either watch their team ball out, or up to 12 hours of random games, but no matter where you look, there are going to be analysts from every walk of life, background, and experience level there to explain, recapitulate, and at times, pull a Lee Corso and drop the "F bomb" on you. But it's ok, because cursing is just part of football!

While CBS, NBC, and Fox Sports (as well as conference networks) have their shows, the college flagship program comes from the mothership, and that's College GameDay on ESPNU.

College Game Day has been on air since 1987, and debuted with Corso, Tim Brando, and Beano Cook as its cast. In 2013, College Game Day will mark its 27th season, with a stellar cast of Chris Fowler, Lee Corso, Kirk Herbstreit, Desmond Howard, David Pollack, and Samantha Steele Ponder, who replaced Erin Andrews when she left ESPN in the summer of 2011, for Fox Sports.

Melissa Stark is one of the main ladies at NFL Network, along with Michelle Beisner, Lindsay Rhodes, Alex Flanagan (previously discussed), Aditi Kinkhabwala, and Rebecca Haarlow – to name a few. Of course, in true NFL Network fashion, they have also employed many retired NFL players to make up its brass, including Warren Sapp, Heath Evans, Donovan McNabb, Randy Moss, and Willie McGinest.

FOX Sports/Fox Sports 1 is becoming stiff competition for ESPN, but in all honesty some of the best news reporting comes via Twitter, and surprisingly, through sports parody accounts.

A friend of mine runs the Not SportsCenter (@NOTSportsCenter) Twitter account, and while it's not a conventional approach, the account and website delivers the major headlines throughout the day with the most concise, and unbiased commentary around.

Fans have been expressing their contempt for preferential and non-stop ad nauseum mentions of one team, or athlete around the clock, and this is largely why fans are taking to Twitter as their primary news source. Let's just say, that if the set walls of

SportsCenter could talk, parody accounts and 140-character armchair analysis could give award-winning narration.

There are a few female sports-savvy journalists I know personally, who are definitely worth mentioning, including Jenna Laine (@JennaLaineBucs), a freelance journalist from Tampa/St. Petersburg, Florida, and University of South Florida alumni. While her specialty is the Tampa Bay Buccaneers, she's one of the best in the business when discussing all things, NFL. Jenna is a member of the Football Writers Association of America, and the Association for Women in Sports Media.

Elika Sadeghi (@steakNstiffarms) has an MBA from Ohio State University, and while her background is in marketing, she has worked for ESPN, with several appearances on Jim Rome's show on CBS, and in the summer of 2013, she was named to Athlon's List of "50 Twitter Accounts Every College Football Fan Should Follow".

Conclusion

The goal for *The Modern Girl's Guide to the Gridiron*, was to be an outside-the-box, no-holds-barred explanation on football, and all that it entails. If you're reading this, congratulations, you survived.

In my three years as a strictly sports journalist, I have had to come up with some crazy shit to describe this game to people. But nothing is more rewarding, than knowing my insane analogies, or hard-witted explanations are helping people learn the game I fell in love with as a kid.

I know that many of you likely purchased this book up under pretenses based on the introduction, that it was going to be easy. But just as athletes push their bodies each and every day through their grueling training regimens to make the game what it is, I wanted to create that same effect with your mind.

If there is one piece of advice I could give you after finishing *The Modern Girl's Guide to the Gridiron*, is that this season, and for the rest of your football loving life, I hope you always remember that your football knowledge is the best accessory you could ever wear on Game Day. But just in case you need a refresher, don't forget to slip a copy in your Louis Vuitton (or NFL- regulation-sized bag) next to the champagne.

Peace, Love, and Touchdowns,

VF Castro

Rules of Engagement

One of the biggest reasons why I was compelled to write this book, was to help combat some of the nonsensical, and outright ridiculous things I see daily, happening on the backend of the game. Racism, affairs, jersey chasing, and women who make it their mission to get impregnated by athletes… you name it, I've seen or heard it all.

I've come across a lot of women who were former NFL girlfriends at one point, and it was usually a 50/50 on how they handled themselves during his struggle. Many had that "magnetic" pull to the business, and understood the level of pressure their men were under. These women targeted their focus on transactions and networking with as many people as they could, to make sure they had all the news to deliver as it was happening, as opposed to hearing things, seeing them online, or when the team was being briefed.

I'm not in the business to air dirty laundry. I'm here to educate and enlighten, so based on my personal observations and stories I've been told by both sides, here are a few cardinal rules that every girl should live by:

- With the exception of League professionals, analysts, media, or agents, nobody needs to know the League's pay scale for athletes, which is why it was omitted from this book, with the exception of Rule No. 6 (below). I don't care what anyone says, nobody has the right to ask an athlete how much money his contract is worth; the second a woman brings this up, the floodgates fly open for speculation. The only exemptions to this rule are business/financial advisors, or committed wives and mothers at the discretion of the athlete.

- If you act like a jersey chaser or a gold digger, you will be treated as such. Sure, the athlete might enjoy what he's seeing for the time being, and a few gifts might be given, but athletes can sniff JC's out pretty well, and they rarely make it that far. As social media platforms expand, the likelihood of your name and probability of photos to surface on the Internet for engaging in any act with an athlete increases exponentially. Learn from the lessons of mistakes past, and act accordingly.

- Never say, "Athletes are unattainable." They're people too, and want to be treated normally. If you're attracted to their physique, there's nothing wrong with it! Just always remember to act like a classy, respectable, intelligent woman, and you'll command their attention at some point or another – and for the right reasons.

- Don't ever ask them about work. It was explained to me like this: "Do you think a guy who works at Burger King making Whoppers all day is going to want to make more, or explain how they're made when he gets home?" That's a big N-O.

- "Gold Diggers" (according to some of the athletes themselves) usually try getting pregnant right out of the gate. The way child support works for athletes, is that the judge bases payments on monthly salary and fixes them. So say a player is making league minimum, (which is $390,000), divide that by 17 weeks, and you're talking about roughly $22,941 a month in salary. Whatever percentage of child support that's taken from his salary is obviously annoying to the player, but they usually accept the terms and move on. But the problem, as discussed earlier, is that 78 percent of these athletes will either be bankrupt, or be in severe financial stress within

~ Rules of Engagement ~

two years after retiring. So while replacing birth control with a placebo in hopes of a payday might sound like a "brilliant" idea, there's a higher chance the athlete will be bankrupt before the child is seven years old. Suggestion to the women tempted by this, if finding a rich athlete is the plan, and you end up with a seven-year, near million-dollar payout, how financially ruined would you be by the time that kid reached 18? It's a lot of money to blow through, but athletes can, have, and will continue to do it in shorter amounts of time than that. Also, state taxes have to be factored in, as paychecks are taxed by the rate each game on the schedule is played in, unless the state doesn't have an income tax, like Florida.

- As a rule, athletes don't like to talk because most live in fear that their words and actions will be used against them, so never tell anyone things you've heard players say, and do NOT say their names. There are better ways to resolve conflicts, or get points across.

- Brides, I'm sorry, but somebody has to say it: please try and refrain from having a wedding during football season. Your wedding is supposed to be your day, and more often than not, if you have your special day during the season, half your guests – even the women – will be more focused on the GameCast on their cell phones, than your nuptial ceremonies. And yes, your guests will be talking shit behind your back because of your decision. I didn't write this rule, but it should be enforced.

- Something I notice enough to present as an issue, is how families and friends act when an athlete goes undrafted. Often, in the later rounds, the athlete starts to lose hope, and it should be the responsibility of his associates to keep him focused. Chances are, his agent is on the phone arranging workouts that family and friends are completely unaware of. Most casual spectators have no clue how teams arrange their draft boards, and trades throughout the draft can, and will affect where he goes. Please be respectful of the process; crying, cursing, and bashing teams, personnel, and agents does not reflect well on the player, and it certainly won't help his spirits.

- Unfortunately, racism still exists in America, and it's a belief system that still circulates throughout our landscape. The problem with racism in football, (or any other team-building centered module) is that at a young age, kids are taught to hate the very guys they might have to protect later on in life. On either side of the ball, you have 11 hearts beating as one, 10 players responding to the calls of one, and a team behind him, that no matter what deodorant he wore that day, or body wash he used, at the end of it all, they smell the same. Their blood looks the same, and they're getting injuries treated by physicians who show no preferential treatment based on their color of their patients skin. It's a different set of politics from high school and down, because you're taught largely the same beliefs as the rest of the guys you play with. If a player is good enough to advance and play college ball and he comes from a racially charged background – no matter what college he steps foot on – it is inevitable that within a few short weeks, he will be brothers with the guys who have the skin color he was raised to hate. The only way to prevent this from happening, is by not participating.

Whether he's a Caucasian QB handing off to an African American RB, or a Haitian guard blocking for an Irish TE; an Indian, Asian, Mexican, Arab, or Inuit on the roster, racism has zero room on the field, and it starts at home. If a child is barred from playing because of this, they're barred from many life experiences.

Glossary

- ***3-Point Stance***: this is formation made by RB's and offensive linemen, in which all of their body weight is evenly distributed to their feet, and one hand

- ***3-4 Defense***: when there are three linemen, and four linebackers

- ***4-3 Defense***: when there are four linemen and three linebackers

- ***46 Defense***: is a 4-3 Defense created by Buddy Ryan (former NFL coach, and Bears defensive coordinator from '78-'85), and made popular by the Chicago Bears (who beat the Patriots 46-10) in Super Bowl 20 on January 26, 1986. It involves a lot of shifting, but pretty much means when the linebackers shift to the offenses weak side, with the DB's (two CB's and one SS) crowding the line of scrimmage. The FS hangs in the backfield like he'd normally do

- ***Audible***: is when the QB changes the play at the line of scrimmage

- ***Backfield***: are the offensive players who line up behind the line of scrimmage, and behind the lineman or linebackers

- ***Bootleg***: when the QB fakes a hand-off to a RB while running in opposite directions of each other, to run, or pass the football

- ***Bubble Screen***: is when the QB takes the snap and throws it directly to a WR (middle/slot/slit)

- ***Burner/Stinger***: is when the network of nerves along the spinal chord stretch, or compress, causing sharp pains and a tingle that extends across the shoulder and down to the arms, but never both at the same time. This causes numbness, and weakness, but is typically isolated and disappears after a few minutes

- *Blitz*: this is when the defense – specifically the linebackers – charge into the offensive backfield with an objective to sack the QB, or rush the pass

- *Blue Chip*: a top prospect student-athlete

- *CBA*: the NFL's Collective Bargaining Agreement is between the Players' Association (NFLPA) and NFL Owners, and is a 10-year agreement involving salary cap, player safety, health benefits, season length, free agency guidelines, revenue sharing, financial transparency, TV contracts, and revenue sharing

- *Clip*: a clip is when an opponent is blocked across the legs, and from behind, resulting in a 15-yard penalty

- *Coffin Corner*: the two corners in the endzone, where the pylons are

- *Contact Period*: a time period when recruiters can have contact with the recruit, and his parents

- *Cover 2*: when both Safeties cover their half of an (imaginary) split backfield

- *Cover 3*: when two Cornerbacks and one Safety occupy their respective 1/3 of the defensive backfield

- *Cut*: when a player changes the direction he is running, very quickly

- *Dead Ball*: when a play is over, or the ball is no longer in play

~ Glossary ~

- **Dead Period**: when there is absolutely zero contact whatsoever, under any circumstance

- **Defensive Holding**: when a defensive player holds or tackles an offensive player who it isn't the ball carrier

- **Delay of Game**: if the ball isn't snapped by the center within the time allotted, they get hit with a Delay of Game, which results in a 5-yard penalty across the board

- **Dime**: this is the same as the Nickel Defense, except that two DB's are brought into the backfield, replacing two LB's. This is to increase personnel on desperate offensive situations to fortify pass protection. These additions to the backfield are called Dime Backs because two nickels equal a dime

- **Draw**: Is when a QB drops back and looks like he's going to pass, then either hands the ball to a RB, or keeps it and runs it himself

- **Drop Back**: when a QB drops back a few yards in the pocket, after the snap to set up the pass

- **Encroachment**: when a player crosses the Line of Scrimmage – or Neutral Zone – to make contact with an opponent prior to the snap, resulting in a 5-yard penalty. I reiterate, "make contact" because this is commonly confused with Offsides and Neutral Zone

- **Facemask**: there really isn't a way to describe this, but it's when an opponent grabs another players' facemask. It's a little more complex, however, as there are two different types: Incidental, which is when it's immediately released, and only results in a 5-yarder. Then there's flagrant, which is when a player purposely grabs the facemask, and pulls his opponent down with it. This not only results in a 15-yarder, but it's also extremely dangerous

~ Glossary ~

- *Fade*: when a receiver runs by the sideline (usually by the endzone) to make the catch, which is typically thrown over, or near the receivers head

- *Fair Catch*: is when the returner motions that he will not be advancing the football

- *Fake Field Goal*: Is a trick play, and the same as a Fake Punt, except for the procedure. The ball is snapped back as it normally would, except either the PK, or Holder drops back and (hopefully) passes it to a receiver for the 6, as opposed to the 3

- *Fake Punt*: is a punt, without the punt. Huh? Ok, so imagine all the procedures of the punt: how they line up, and under what circumstances. Well, when it's a fake punt, the punter either runs it downfield, or passes it off to a receiver. It's rare, and designed to exploit weaknesses in defenses, but it's an act of desperation

- *False Start*: when a member of the Offense moves before the ball is snapped, which results in a 5-yard penalty

- *Flats*: the flats run from the line of scrimmage, along the central hash-marks, and 10-yards downfield

- *Flea Flicker*: when the QB hands the ball to a RB, who pitches the ball backwards and laterally (east/west) to the QB before the line of scrimmage

- *Franchise Tag*: Is used on a player who is valuable to the team, and can be done in two ways: Exclusive (a one-year tag equal to the salaries of the top five players at his position, or 120 percent more than what he received the previous year), or Non-Exclusive which carry the same stipulations, but allows the player to act as a restricted free agent. If another team wants him, his original team has to match terms or give the new team two first-round draft picks

~ Glossary ~

- *Free Kick*: is when a catch is fairly made by the receiving team, and they elect to attempt a FG from where the ball was spotted dead

- *Gunner*: is the fastest player on the team, and usually a WR, CB, or Safety. Not to be confused with Gunslinger, which is the QB

- *Hail Mary*: is a play of last resort, and usually a bomb pass to the endzone.

- *Helmet-To-Helmet Hit*: an illegal act, when two helmets collide, with emphasized target on a defenseless player

- *Hip Flexors*: are the three muscles that give flexion to the hip

- *Hip Pointers*: are usually caused by tackling, which result in a bone bruise or in more serious cases, a fracture to the pelvis

- *Horse-Collar Tackle*: when a defender (not to be confused with a member on the Defense) tackles his opponent by grabbing the back of his neck between the helmet and shoulder pads/collar area

- *Icing The Kicker*: means that when a kicking team is dialing in and waiting for the snap, the opposing HC calls a timeout. This is intended to make the kicker nervous on his second attempt, but rarely does

- *Illegal Crack Back*: is when an offensive player (usually a receiver or RB) who is outside the formation, go in motion on the snap and run to block an unsuspecting defensive tackle near the line of scrimmage. If contact is made above the waist, or 5+ yards down field, it's legal. If it's below the waist, or on the LOS, it's illegal and a 15-yard penalty

- *Illegal Forward Pass*: is a pass thrown from past the line

~ Glossary ~

of scrimmage after changing possession (from QB to ball carrier, typically). This results in a loss of a down, and a 5-yard penalty from the spot of the foul. Ex: If penalty were marked at the 45-yard line on 3rd and 6, the offense would be on a 4th and 51, and be forced to punt

- *Illegal Formation*: seven or more players are required to line up at the line of scrimmage for at least one second before the ball is snapped. If not, it results in a 5-yarder

- *Illegal Shift*: is an infraction against the offense, where players move, or shift before the snap, by changing positions and failing to reestablish, or reset and hold for at least a second after

- *"In The Bubble"*: refers to a player who is being evaluated by performance who is on the fence. This term is used a lot in pre-season when rosters are being trimmed

- *Injured Reserve*: is a retainer "list" a player is put on when he can't play due to an injury, while freeing up a spot for another player. Older rules were that when a player was put on IR, he was out for the season, but In August 2012, the NFL and NFLPA reached an agreement that allowed a player to return to the 53-man roster after 6 weeks, and be activated after 8 weeks

- *Interception*: when a member of the opposite team catches the ball during a forward pass

- *Interference*: when a player illegally prevents an opposing player from being able to catch a pass

- *Juke*: a move by a ball carrier that's intended to deceive or trick an opponent to avoid a tackle

- *Kneel*: is when a player – usually the QB – takes a knee that ends the play. This can happen in any situation, but usually before halftimes, or when the winning team wants to end the game – called a "victory formation"

~ Glossary ~

- *Lateral*: Is when the ball is pitched (thrown) backwards and lateral (east/west) to another player

- *"Late On His Reads"*: means that a QB is hesitant, and literally late reading his personnel to get the ball off

- *Letter of Intent*: (NLI), is a legally binding contract between the player and the institution through the NCAA, that declares where he will be attending, and playing college football

- *Live Ball*: when a ball is in play

- *Lockout (NFL)*: lasted from March 12, 2011 – July 25th, 2011. Both sides were unable to come to an agreement on the new CBA (before the expiration {March 3} and extension {March 11} of the previous CBA), locking players out of facilities. They couldn't receive playbooks, meet with team doctors or trainers, or have any contact with coaches or staff members. There was no free agency period, and it wasn't until July 30, 2011 that the lockout officially ended, when NFL Commissioner Roger Goodell, and NFLPA Executive Director DeMaurice Smith signed the new agreement

- *Man-To-Man Coverage*: Is when each member of the defense is assigned to individually cover each player on the offense

- *Move The Chains*: an archaic – yet indisputable – unit of measuring 10-yard increments, starting at the original Line of Scrimmage

- *Muff*: is a loose ball that gets dropped, typically on a punt return, or kickoff return

- *Multiple Receiver Set*: is a component in the Spread, which is designed as a "run first" offense. It just means that there are multiple WR's

~ Glossary ~

- **Neutral Zone Infraction**: when a player lines up past the line of scrimmage

- **Nickel**: this is a play strategically designed to stop the pass, and is when a fifth DB replaces a linebacker. Again, DB's are in the defensive backfield covering WR's, typically. This addition to the backfield is called The Nickel Back

- **Offensive Holding**: when a player on the offense uses his hands (mainly) to "hold" a defender, preventing him from advancing to the ball carrier

- **Offsides**: when a player crosses the line of scrimmage resulting in a 5-yard penalty

- **Onside Kick**: is when the kicking team attempts to retrieve their own ball after it's kicked off. If the kick goes out of bounds, the receiving team takes possession. In CFB, the kick must move 10-yards, and bounce twice

- **Option**: you will hear this a lot during games, but all it means is that the QB is pulling out all the tricks, and pissing off defenders

- **Outside**: the area on the field closest to the sidelines

- **Overtime**: when the game is tied after 60 minutes of regulation in NFL/CFB/CFL, and 48 in HS

- **Pass Block**: Is when the o-line creates a wall to push defenders back, or stop them so the QB can pass the ball

- **Pass Rush**: when defensive players attempt to get to the quarterback and make a tackle, before he makes a pass

- **Pass Protection**: when the OL blocks for the QB, to protect him on passing plays

- **Pass Interference**: Is when a player (usually on the defense, although offensive PI occurs) interferes with

~ Glossary ~

another players' ability to catch a fair pass, and results in a 15-yard penalty on defensive PI, and 10-yards on offensive PI

- *Play Action*: when a QB fakes a handoff to a RB, then fires it when he sees his eligible receiver open downfield

- *Pick*: is the same as an interception, however, when this happens it's referred to as "… he was picked off"

- *Post Route*: is when the ball is thrown to a receiver, who takes off in the middle of the field. Hence "post", as in "goal posts"

- *Pocket*: this is the 1,600-1,800 pound wall of O-Linemen body mass that protects the QB

- *Pooch Kick*: is a kick that is intentionally hit without full power

- *Pump Fake*: is a move by the QB to trick defenses into thinking he has thrown the football in one direction, but pulls the ball in, and throws it in another direction

- *Pylon*: the orange markers in all four corners of the endzone

- *Quarterback Rating*: a number indicating how effective and accurate a QB is

- *Quarterback Sneak*: is typically a short-yardage situation, where the QB takes the snap, then advances the football himself, by a pass, or running

- *Quiet Period*: a 42-day period from September through November when recruits can visit campuses, and coaches can have in-person off campus visits with recruits

- *Redshirt*: a college player who skips a year of football (usually for medical or academic reasons) without losing

~ Glossary ~

a year of eligibility. RS Freshmen are in their second year academically, but their second season

- **Red Zone**: this isn't just an Old Spice Men's deodorant; it's an imaginary line (or red shaded, and provided by Verizon if you're watching the NFL at home), which marks the defenses 20-yard line to the goal line. Referring back to Tebow, this is where the majority of his scoring magic happens

- **Roughing the Passer**: when a player smacks into the quarterback after the ball has been released

- **Roughing the Kicker**: is when a defensive player makes contact with any of the members on the kicking unit (Place Kicker, Punter, Holder)

- **Routes**: in themselves are practically buffet tables on a playbook, but they're designed for WR's to run to get open for a pass

- **Run Block**: is when members of the offense "bull rush" the defense, creating holes for RB's on running plays

- **Sack**: Is when the ball carrier gets taken down when trying to throw a forward pass

- **Safety Blitz**: there really is no other way to put this, than an all out assault by both the strong safety, and free safety to hit the shit out of the QB

- **Scramble**: is when the QB runs around the backfield (behind the line of scrimmage), to avoid the pass rush, and buy more time to hit receivers

- **Secondary**: this is the defensive backfield, and comprised of two Safeties, and two Cornerbacks

- **Screen**: a short forward pass when the defense has blitzed the QB, allowing the OL to block for the RB

~ Glossary ~

- **Shotgun**: when the QB takes the snap from several yards behind the line of scrimmage
- **Slant**: when the ball carrier runs the field at an angle
- **Slot**: refer back to the Gap Assignments (C), which is a gap between the WR's and Tackles
- **Slot Receiver**: is a third WR who isn't used frequently, but plays on the inside (middle of the field)
- **Sneak**: is used on short yardage situations, and when the QB advances the ball forward
- **Spearing**: is the intentional use of a helmet and facemask to hurt an opponent with the sole purpose of inflicting pain by any means, and very much illegal
- **Stutter Step**: is a footwork technique, when a player slows down but keeps moving. The defender thinks he has a tackle, but the ball carrier jukes, then quickly regains speed and momentum
- **Squib Kick**: is a ball that's kicked low to the ground on purpose
- **Tampa 2**: is a defensive strategy adopted and made popular by the Tampa Bay Buccaneers during the Tony Dungy coaching era. To execute this properly, MLB's drop back creating a Cover 3 in the backfield to cover deep routes better. Players are assigned to protect their respective gaps, tackle, and be fast as hell while doing it
- **Three and Out**: when the offense is forced to punt on fourth down because they can't get a first down in the first three plays of a drive
- **Turf Toe**: a sprain that occurs at the base of the big toe
- **Two-Point Conversion**: in the event a TD has been made and a team decides to "go for two", this is what it's called.

~ Glossary ~

The offense sets up like they would on any other down and hopes the ball carrier either crosses the plane, or the QB hits his target. This is riskier than the PAT, but single points will win football games

- **Two-Minute Warning**: is just that. A warning that is given at the end of the second, and fourth quarters, and regardless of play, the clock stops

- **Walk On**: refers to College Football, and is a player who is on the team, but not on scholarship

- **Weak Side**: on offense: the opposite side of the field where the TE's are

- **Wheel Route**: is when a receiver travels parallel along the line of scrimmage, and proceeds up field after the reception

- **Zone Coverage**: when defensive players are assigned to cover specific parts on the field – mainly DB's and LB's

Thank You

To my momma, Norma Castro, and brother, David E. Castro. I love you both; Dad would be so proud. Renee Schivo, my best friend and sister... thanks for dragging me to Texas! Marketing guru, and my amazing friend Elika Sadeghi. Camie Cragg and Kylie Keenan at Camie Cragg Fitness in Reno, Nevada. Shannon "Decker" Henderson. The Johnson's and Bristol's for your compassion when my father was dying. Ed Levy, and Alma Gonzales – you were angels to my father in his last months; thank you for everything. Jose Pinon, Jr. for bringing out the best in my mother, and passing it on to me. Sue and Ron Duncan for the sunset photo. John Bender. The University of Nevada Wolf Pack. Alex Holmes, and the University of Southern California Football Program. Texas Tech University Football. The Human Bean, Reno. Starbucks on Keystone. EDM on BPM. Alesso, Krewella, Swedish House Mafia, Dada Life, Avicii, Rihanna, and Avenged Sevenfold. Jessica Hicks, Jenay Duckett, and Veronica Chavez at MAC – Reno. Kris Hughes at Rant Sports for the opportunity to put my crazy voice to CFB. My amazing lawyer, Cathy Tische, thank you for your guidance throughout this process. Everyone who anonymously contributed to this book, because they believed in me. My first agent, Travis Bell. And the city of Austin, Texas for inspiring me.

To the members of law enforcement, military servicemen and women, and their families – still with us, and those who have passed – I sincerely thank you. Your sacrifices, acts of valor, and courage allow us the freedom to enjoy our beloved pastimes – like football – in comfort and safety.

Acknowledgements

Creative Director/Designer (web, covers, illustrations)/Developer: David E. Castro

Photography: Jeramie Lu, Jeramie Lu Photography, Reno, Nevada

Hair: Shannon Henderson at Shear Bliss Salon, Reno, Nevada

Makeup: Jenay Duckett at MAC Cosmetics, The Summit, Reno, Nevada

Content Edits: Brandon Folsom at SB Nation and MLive, and Amber Davies, Professional/College Scout with the Houston Texans – thank you!